THE DINKUM AUSSIE DICTIONARY

THE DINKUM AUSSIE DICTIONARY

Crooked Mick of the Speewa

How to get stuck into this book

Some of the words and expressions listed in this book are derogatory and may cause offence. Those that fall into this category are indicated by '(derog.)'. We do not recommend that you use such words and expressions, but we have nevertheless included them as this is a book about language usage, for better or worse.

Italics are used for foreign expressions, sometimes for emphasis, and to indicate all words and expressions that have a separate listing.

Sadly, the author – the legendary Crooked Mick of the Speewa – is no longer with us. In fact, he's carked it. But his work lives on, and you can read about him on page 35.

In the spirit of Crooked Mick, we say, "Have a bonzer geek at this little book".

The Editor

A

A Bex, a nice cup of tea and a good lie down

A somewhat archaic phrase, usually directed by a woman friend to a woman sufferer. In the past the victim's husband would have usually just beaten her up and stolen her housekeeping money to get on the *grog* and go to the races. In these trying times the victim will probably have discovered that her husband has turned gay. The amazing Bex headache powder, not being what it once was, due to changes in the pharmaceutical laws of the land, is no longer of much use. The victim is normally advised to skip the lie down as well, and flee simultaneously to her lawyer and the nearest women's refuge.

ABC, The

The Australian Broadcasting Corporation, also affectionately known as 'Aunty'.

A bit strong

A hurtful remark or action, for example, "Well, I can understand him pissing off with your *missus,* but taking the dog as well, now that was a bit strong".

About right

Means that the statement/fact is absolutely correct. The phrase is an excellent example of the average Australian's refusal or inability to admit anything being true except in an indirect manner. Thus the reply to the classic phrase, "I think therefore I am,' is: "That'd be about right, *mate*".

Aerial pingpong
Australia's home-devised football code, Australian Rules. Incomprehensible to civilised races, it makes about as much sense as the equally dubious sport of water polo. Commonly known as *Aussie Rules*.

Akubra
An Australian brand of hat that comes in a wide range of styles and generally features a broad brim. Golfer Greg Norman wears one, as do country people all over Australia. The name is believed to be derived from an Aboriginal word, meaning, appropriately, 'hat'.

Alf
Rather archaic now, but once a popular term for a fool. An Alf is always an *ocker*.

Alice, The
The Outback town of Alice Springs, at the heart of *The Red Centre*.

All dressed up and nowhere to go
The person referred to as being in this state has made a mistake about the time of a plane departure, the day of the party, a sure thing at the races, or even the fact that the world cared about him or her. In male parlance it means that one has been 'stood up' by one's *sheila*. A failure.

All over him/her like a rash

Meaning unable to keep one's hands off the object of one's desire – for example, "She was all over him like a rash at the *pub* last night".

Amber fluid

One of the many names for beer or 'suds'.

Ankle biter

A form of *rug rat*. A member of the human race, of indeterminate sex and colour, under two years of age.

ANZAC

Acronym for the Australian and New Zealand Army Corps, the *diggers* of which performed heroic deeds for the British during World War I. The non-capitalised 'Anzac' is frequently seen in conjunction with words such as 'Street', 'Square', 'Parade', 'Bridge', 'biscuit', etc.

Apeshit

Stark raving mad, usually in the noun form, for example: "He's apeshit today".

Apple Isle, The

The island state of Tasmania, so-named because the cool (some would say freezing) climate is conducive to growing apples. Also known as *Tassie*.

Are you right?

Not a question regarding correctness, but a query as to someone's welfare, or an offer of assistance – as in "Are you right (pronounced 'roight'), love?" addressed to a waiting customer by a saleswoman. *See also* YOU'RE RIGHT.

Arse about with care
Means that things have gone wrong because some fool has tried to help. In other words the building is not only a gutted ruin but the members of the local fire brigade have destroyed the remnants with their hoses.

Arse into gear
One should get one's arse into gear – get moving, get active – if one is not about to get *arseholed*. The necessity of at least appearing to do some work while the boss is around.

Arseholed
Has nothing to do with the Americanism 'asshole' which means a fool or a curmudgeon and everything to do with losing one's job (if a bricklayer) or being thrown out of a *pub* (if one is a lower-order drunk who is arseholed). Chairmen of Directors do not get arseholed from their jobs; they are sacked. Likewise, they are thrown out of public houses. There are certain fine points of language in this egalitarian society.

Arthur or Martha
Someone who 'doesn't know if he's Arthur or Martha' is in a state of chronic confusion.

Arvo
Afternoon, as in "See *youse* Sat'd'y arvo". A common example of the Australian obsession with abbreviation.
'This afternoon' is 'sarvo'.

As game as Ned Kelly
See NED KELLY.

As thick as two bricks/planks
Describes someone of breath taking stupidity.

As useful as...

A starting phrase that can precede almost any collection of words meaning that the person concerned is not pulling his or her weight and is making no useful contribution to the philosophical discussion at hand. Thus, "as useful as a wether at a ram sale", "as useful as tits on a bull", "as useful as an ashtray on a motorbike", and last but not least, "as useful as a glass door on a *dunny*".

Aussie

The Australian name for an Australian person, or some times for the country itself. People from *O.S.* often incorrectly pronounce the word as 'Awsee' – it should be 'Ozzie'.

Aussie Rules

The game of Australian Rules Football, also known as AFL (Australian Football League) and *aerial pingpong,* which is a total mystery not only to foreigners, but most people from New South Wales, the Australian Capital Territory and southern Queensland, where rugby is play d. The game is an Australian adaptation of Gaelic football.

Aussie salute

See GREAT AUSTRALIAN SALUTE.

'Ave a go

A cry of encouragement, meaning 'stop standing around and do something, you lazy *bastard*' (a form of *barracking),* generally heard at sporting events and normally followed by 'ya mug!' *See also* MUG.

Back o' Bourke
(derog.) An expression describing somewhere remote and inaccessible. Bourke is a small town in *Outback* New South Wales. 'The back of beyond' has the same meaning.

Backblocks
Much the same as *Back o' Bourke,* 'the back of beyond' and *Woop Woop.*

Bad way
One is in a bad way if one is suffering from a hangover or has been recently run over by a double-decker bus.

Bag
To criticise or 'knock' someone or something.
See also KNOCKER.

Baked dinner
Once the traditional Sunday midday meal, consisting of a roast leg of lamb, roast and mashed spuds, roast pumpkin, carrot and parsnip, peas, brown gravy and mint sauce. Prepared by the expert hands of the average Australian housewife, it was once guaranteed to *choke a brown dog.*

Balmain bug
A tasty and good-looking crustacean related to the lobster and the true crayfish. A shining example of the Australian inability to give good food a pleasant name. In a displaced burst of northern nationalism, Queenslanders insist on calling the wretched animal the Moreton Bay bug.

Bananabender

A person from sunny Queensland, where bananas and other tropical fruits abound. Normally used disparagingly.

Bangs like a dunny door in a gale

Used by males in reference to any female of the species who is said to be free with her sexual favours. It invariably turns out to be a lie.

Barbie

A barbecued meal, cooked on a hotplate or over hot coals. Regarded with universal scorn by those who slaver over *bistecca alla Fiorentina,* which is exactly the same thing apart from the fact that it is done indoors and served by some *wanker* in a dinner jacket.

Barcoo rot

A form of scurvy caused by the bushworker's diet of corned beef and *damper.*

Barra

Abbreviation of the Aboriginal word 'barramundi' – a giant perch found in tropical waters and famed for its succulent flesh.

Barrack

To encourage one's team from the sidelines, not always in complimentary terms, e.g.: "Get in there and fight, you bunch of *bloody mongrels*". See also 'AVE A GO.

Barry Crocker

A good example of Australian rhyming slang – one that is used particularly in sporting parlance to describe a 'shocker', as in "I had a Barry Crocker of a match". The opposite of this is a *blinder.*

Bastard

Either a term of affection as in, 'good old bastard', a term of abuse as in, '*bloody* bastard', or a comment on the weather as in, 'bastard of a day', meaning that it is either hot or cold. The Australian male uses the word indiscriminately in place of almost any other in the English language, thus:

"So I told the flash bastard I wasn't going to do his bastard of a job on a bastard of a day like this. But the bastard told me I had no *bloody* choice. I did it and he turned out not to be a bad old bastard in the end. But it was still a bastard of a job".

The one meaning that the word does not carry in Australian usage is its officially defined one concerning the legitimacy of one's birth. In general 'flash bastard' means a *smart-arse*, 'good old bastard' is a close friend and 'poor old bastard' applies to a person of the grandfather class who is down on his luck.

Bastard from the bush

Mythical folk hero celebrated (mainly) in smutty jingles and at least one long, sub-literate poem. The *bastard* from the *bush* is one of life's great swine and, because of this, tolerated with great affection by Australian *blokes*.

Bathers

A bathing costume, can be called 'swimmers' —
see also COZZIE *and* TOGS.

Battler

Someone who has had a hard life and will continue to have one due to unforeseen circumstances, his or her own stupidity, or both. Battlers are generally hard workers of abstemious habits but these twin decencies never get them anywhere. The expression *little Aussie battler* means much the same.

Bazz/Bazza
Originally a cartoon character but now taken to mean your average, knockabout, sub-literate Australian *bloke*. In other words, more or less a fool.

Be in the chair
One of an infinite number of drinking express ions. This one means to be the person in a group of drinkers (or a *school*) whose turn it is to *stand,* or *shout,* or buy, a round of drinks.

Beats watering the garden
A pleasantry uttered by one who has been engulfed by a flood.

Beaut
Very good or excellent. Normally used in the phrases, 'you beaut', 'you bloody beaut', or the television corruption, *'bewdie'.*

Better than a poke in the eye with a burnt stick
Things have turned out better than expected but in a backhanded sort of way the car, by some miracle, has not been repossessed and one's house has not burnt down.

Bewdie
See BEAUT.

Big Australian, The
Broken Hill Proprietary Company Limited (BHP), Australia's largest and oldest mining and heavy manufacturing company.

Big smoke
A country expression for any large city.

Billabong
A waterhole formed by a broken meander of a river.

Billy

The name of a friend or a pot for boiling water for tea over an open fire. In the case of the former it must not be black. In the case of the latter it has to be. A shiny billy makes awful tea.

Billy tea

Tea made in a *billy*.

Billy-o

An archaic word that can mean that one had a wonderful time at a party or that one is feeling more than slightly off-colour or sick; thus, "I played up like billy-o last night' or, "my rheumatism is playing up like billy-o". One's rheumatism, sciatica or mild case of clap can also be "giving one billy-o". One can also give the neighbour's unpleasant dog billy-o which translates into the fact that one has beaten the wretched animal half to death with a pick handle.

Bite your bum!

Often used to tell someone to shut up, go away, get lost, etc.

Bitzer

A dog consisting of many breeds, a mongrel. Bits of this and bits of that.

Black bastard

A term of endearment used to describe Australia's only home-bred dog strain (other than the disputed *kelpie*), officially known as the *blue heeler,* Queensland blue or Queensland cattle dog. All blues are regarded by their owners as being *as thick as two bricks* but *as game as Ned Kelly.* They are also renowned for their biting ability.

Black Maria

A 'paddy wagon', or a prison cell on four wheels that, if necessary, can travel at high speeds. In the past most of its business was done outside *pubs* on Saturday nights. These days its customers also come from the street demonstration set.

Black Stump

The official signpost at the beginning of nowhere the *Outback*. A solid version of the Styx which lacks Charon as a ticket collector. Anyone who lives 'beyond the Black Stump' is regarded as being stark raving mad.

Blind

You've had so much, you can't even see, let alone think. 'Blind drunk' expresses the same noble sentiments.

Blind Freddy

A mythical and dull person who can understand matters intellectual only if they are hammered into his skull by a railway fettler using an old-fashioned 10-inch spike. Thus, "Even Blind Freddy could tell you', that the government would fall, that the river was about to flood, etc.

Blinder

A stunning display of sporting prowess, as in "He had a blinder and scored three goals".

Bloke

A man, guy or fellow. A bloke is the sort of person you'd call *mate,* for better or worse.

Blood bin

Where footballers are sent to have their injuries very temporarily patched up. They usually return to the field immediately to have more damage inflicted.
See also SIN BIN.

Bloodhouse

An unsavoury hotel.

Bloody

Once the great Australian adjective, in these intellectual times it has been supplanted by a four letter word with '-ing' attached which describes the act of fornication. Frequently used in conjunction with *bastard,* it is also inserted in sentences where 'bloody' makes even less sense than normal. Often used to emphasise that something is particularly good, thus, '"bloody good feed/ fight/day/night/ party/budgie". It is also used to emphasise bad things, as in "a bloody awful meal/film".

Bloody oath!

A common expression of either wholehearted agreement or complete exasperation. Confusing, I know, but the saying demonstrates yet another use of the great Australian adjective. 'Bleeding oath!' is a variation. *See also* MY OATH.

Blotto

Dead drunk; intoxicated to the extreme.

Blowie

A blowfly.

Blow-in

An unexpected and not particularly welcome guest: "He's just a *bloody* blow-in; tell him to go to *buggery*".

Bludge

To loaf. 'Having a bludge' is an integral part of the Australian working man's life. The word can also mean to scrounge or impose on others.

Bludger
In theory one who lives on the earnings of a prostitute. In actual fact still the worst insult that can be offered a man in Australia, hence, *dole bludger*. This expression is usually mouthed by members of the rabid right in this country against anyone not of their political opinion.

Blue
A dispute, argument or fight – as in "I had a right blue with my boss this *arvo*" (*see also* BUNG ON A BLUE). Blue is also an abbreviation of *blue heeler* and, strangely, a red-headed person.

Blue heeler
See BLACK BASTARD. Also, a police officer.

Bluebottle
A type of stinging jellyfish that frequents Australia's beach waters in summer.

Bluey
A bedroll containing clothing and other odds and ends carried by a *swagman,* also known as a *swag* or a *matilda.*

Bobby-dazzler
Someone or something excellent, as in, "You little bobby-dazzler".

Bob's yer uncle
She's sweet, everything is okay. Thus the Australian reply to a NASA official's query as to the possibility of a space-shuttle lift-off would be: "Bob's yer uncle, *mate*". As this would cause some confusion, Australians by and large are banned from verbal roles in free-world space scenarios.

Bodgie

Once an unwholesome species of lower-order male street life in the 1950s (the female version being a 'Widgie').
Now used only as part of the phrase 'a bodgie job' or 'to bodgie up', meaning that a highly specialised piece of electronic equipment has been lashed together with fencing wire or anything else that happened to be lying around the toolshed at the time.

Bog in

An invitation to sit down at the dinner table and delicately partake of the excellent comestibles prepared by one's hostess.

Bomb out

To fail... "I had a go at the job but I bombed out".

Bonzer

This word, meaning *grouse* or good, is now rarely used, having become a terrible cliché. Formerly, however, after *bogging in* one could have thanked one's hostess by declaring, "That was a bonzer feed, that was". Also spelt 'bonza'.

Boofhead

A former cartoon character noted for his thickness.
In general terms, a dullard.

Boofy

The adjective that relates to *boofhead*.

Bookie

A bookmaker.

Boomer

A large male kangaroo; otherwise something good or successful, as in, "That was a real boomer".

Booze bus

A police vehicle containing *coppers* and equipment for performing random breath tests on drivers. Booze buses lurk unseen by the roadside, ready to entrap hapless drivers who have been on the *piss*.

Boozer

The pub, the *rubbity*. A home for *blokes*.

Borak

To 'poke borak' at someone is to ridicule them. The word is probably from an Aboriginal source.

Boss cocky

Originally a farmer (a *cocky*) who hired labourers, but also used when referring to anyone who is in charge.

Bot

A bot is an annoying person who *cadges* persistently. Also a verb.

Bottle shop

Not a retail outlet that sells glassware – rather a shop stocking beer, wine, spirits and all forms of *grog*. Sometimes called a 'bottle-o', and known elsewhere in the world as an off-licence, liquor store, etc.

Bottler

Not the proprietor of a *bottle shop,* but something or someone inspiring excitement or admiration – as in, "you little bottler!"

Bottom of the harbour

A scheme by which companies were manipulated to thwart the Deputy Commissioner of Taxation of money that was rightfully the property of the Australian Federal government. In the 1970s people who ran bottom of the harbour schemes were regarded by certain sections of the business community as national heroes. They still are.

Bower bird

An Australian native bird that decorates its home with useless glittering items in an effort to entice a female bower bird to share his life. In human terms the description retains its accuracy.

Brass razoo

A worthless item is said to be "not worth a brass razoo". Brass razoos are enthusiastically collected by *bower birds*.

Brick short of a load

Used to describe a simple-minded person, someone who is 'not all there'. *See also* COUPLE OF PIES SHORT OF A GRAND FINAL, KANGAROOS IN THE TOP PADDOCK *and* NOT THE FULL BOTTLE.

Brissie

Brisbane, the laid-back, sub-tropical capital of the state of Queensland. Pronounced 'Brizzie'.

Brumby

A wild horse, which is an integral component of Australia's canned dogfood industry and the advertising business, which, for some peculiar reason, uses herds of brumbies to advertise products like soap powder.

Bub

A common term for a baby.

Bucket

To criticise or in turn be criticised. One can bucket an adversary or, in one's turn, be bucketed.

Buck jumper

A rodeo horse that jumps up and down to earn its daily hay ration for reasons that the beast itself cannot understand.

Buckley's

In unpleasant situations this means that one has no chance whatsoever. No-one knows for sure who the mythical Buckley was. One story holds that he was a convict who escaped and lived with the Aborigines. People in the colony thought he had no chance of survival, hence 'Buckley's'. The name of the Melbourne firm, Buckley and Nunn, is another suggested derivation. Always used in the phrase, "You've got two chances, *mate,* yours and Buckley's".

Budgie

An idiotic and small member of the parrot family – native to Australia's arid regions, and much loved as a pet by elderly women. With patience budgies can be taught almost as many tricks as company directors, doctors and lawyers.

Buggalugs

An affectionate, if somewhat irreverent, Australian equivalent of 'whatsisname'. Very convenient when one is talking about someone whose name has been forgotten – as in "Hey Bruce, where does buggalugs live?" Can also be spelt 'buggerlugs'.

Bugger

Sometimes a substitute for *bastard* inasmuch as one can be a mean old bugger or a good old bugger. One can also have 'bugger all' (nothing) or be told to 'bugger off' (to piss off). As with *bastard* it can also be a bugger of a day or a bugger of a job. Unlike *bastard,* however, one can say *'buggered'* (exhausted), *'buggered* about' (given a hard time by one's *mates* or employer), or *'buggered* if I know' (meaning "I don't have a clue"). The word has absolutely nothing to do with its (Oxford) derivation of a heretic from Bulgaria or a sodomite.

Buggered

A particularly useful Australian *word* – *see* BUGGER.

Buggery

Either a mythical place, as in telling someone to "piss off and go to buggery", or something extreme or excessive: "me leg hurts like buggery".

Bull artist

Short for 'bullshit artist'. An unpleasant liar who is much given to personal boasting about his cleverness. A member of Federal Parliament.

Bulldust

Fine dust that covers vehicle tracks and potholes in the *Outback.* Also something worthless or a lie as in, "That's a *bloody* load of *bloody* bulldust, *mate*".

Bullocky

One in charge of a bullock wagon. Traditionally bullockies were given to hard swearing although why these worthies should be singled out as distinct from the remainder of the male population of the time will forever remain a mystery.

Bull's roar

Insulting expression indicating failure, normally on the sporting field. If something doesn't come within a bull's roar of something else, it can be judged to have 'missed by a mile'. Most expressions of this nature have resisted metrication.

Bumper

A cigarette butt. However, a bumper harvest is not one of fag ends.

Bundy

Bundaberg rum, a popular alcoholic drink manufactured in Bundaberg, Queensland. Bundy comes in UP (underproof: 37.1 per cent) and OP (the lethal overproof: an incredible 57.7 per cent) varieties. *See also* VIRGIN'S RUIN.

Bung

A word with many uses – either (as a verb) to put or throw something somewhere ('bung it in the drawer') or (as an adjective) something that is broken or not in good working order. The latter meaning, from an Aboriginal word, could be used to describe anything from a car to a relationship. *Bunging it on,* however, is completely different.

Bung on a blue

To 'stack on a tum'; with women an attack of hysterics, with men a fist fight. If women bung on a blue by throwing plates or knives they invariably 'turn on the waterworks'. Men, on the other hand, are not supposed to cry.

Bunghole

Cheese.

Bunging it on

To act out of one's own class in the upwardly mobile sense. For instance, if one's host, who is normally given to providing his guests with *fourpenny dark* out of *Vegemite* glasses, suddenly offers a proper champagne out of equally proper glasses, he is said to be 'bunging it on' or 'bunging on side'. Bunging it on is much frowned upon.

Bunyip

A legendary beast of the *bush,* well known to the Aborigines and early white explorers. Now largely replaced by the 'Nullarbor Nymph' and panthers of various colours. In the Antipodean sense it falls into the same category as the Loch Ness monster, the Himalayan yeti and the North American wendigo.

Burl

A burl is an attempt or try at something, or to move quickly *see* GIVE IT A BURL *and* GO FOR A BURL.

Bush, the

An unkempt area of scraggly ground covered with use less gumtrees. Most Australians have as little as possible to do with the bush although they lyingly claim that this is the area where their hearts belong. However, to 'go *bush*' means that one has fled civilisation because of the pressing demands of one's creditors. In a secondary sense it means to have gone mad. In its broadest sense, the bush can be anywhere outside a major town or city.

Bush-bash

To travel through dense or virgin bushland.

Bush telegraph

A mysterious and unofficial form of word-of-mouth communication that operates throughout the *bush*. Also known as the 'bush wireless'.

Bush tucker

Simple native food or *tucker,* found growing or running wild in the *bush.* Aborigines have lived on bush tucker for tens of thousands of years, but the term is now also used to describe some of the fancy offerings of 'Modem Australian' cuisine that are served in expensive city restaurants.

Bushie

One who comes from, or lives in, the *bush.* Often used in a derogatory sense to describe someone who is rather slow-witted, with few social skills and absolutely no fashion sense. Similar to a *Dubbo.*

Bush week

A situation where everything is a *bloody* mess when it shouldn't be, or where something has gone wrong and the perpetrator of the action is taking advantage of the person making the charge: "What do you think this is, *bloody* bush week?" A phrase much used in the country's armed services which normally operate on Murphy's Law (if something can go wrong, it will go wrong).

But

The use of this word to terminate a sentence is a curious Australianism, designed to indicate 'however' or 'though', or used simply as a meaningless ending. An example: "Isn't *Strine* a funny language, but?"

By jingo

An exclamation that indicates affirmation or surprise.

BYO

The acronym for 'Bring Your Own', referring to things such as taking *grog* to parties or unlicensed restaurants, or *snags* to a *barbie.* Also 'BYOG' (Bring Your Own Grog).

C

Cab Sav
Australian for the type of wine known elsewhere as Cabernet Sauvignon.

Cabbie
A taxi or cab driver.

Cactus
If something is cactus, it is useless, *rooted, bung* or dead, as in "The tyre on me *bloody ute's* cactus".

Cadge
To beg, borrow or steal, but in a friendly sort of way. Thus a 'cadger' is a cut above the universally despised *bot*. Cadgers normally ask for things that don't really matter, as in, "Can I cadge a *rollie?*", which translates as "Can I have the necessary ingredients to make myself a roll-your-own-cigarette?"

Camp as a row of tents
Used to describe a raving queer, *poofter* or *shirt-lifter*. A male homosexual.

Cark
To die, as in, "He's carked it". Machinery, especially cars, can also cark it. Also spelt 'kark'.

C'arn!
'Come on' – used mainly by those who are *barracking* for their team or favourite individual in a sporting event. As in "C'arn the Swannies!' or 'C'arn the Bombers!".

Canyon like a pork chop

To overreact or make a fuss about nothing.

Cask

A wine cask (an ingenious Australian invention, incidentally) a cardboard box that houses a bladder containing wine, port, sherry, etc. The advantage of a cask over a bottle is that it's cheaper and holds more grog, as well as making it impossible to assess exactly how much one is drinking. *See also* CHATEAU CARDBOARD.

Charge like a wounded bull

An establishment that has excessively high prices might be said to "Charge like a wounded bull".

Chateau cardboard

Wine from a cheap cardboard *cask,* similar to *plank* and usually of inferior quality.

Cheerio

Australians use cheerio as both a farewell and a greeting. On the radio, for example, an interviewer's guest might send a hello or cheerio to his or her family and friends.

Chesty Bond

A former cartoon and advertising character who specialised in sleeveless singlets and male underwear in general. He was good looking, generally decent and kind to women, children and dogs. Universally despised by the average Australian male who allows his *missus* to buy his underwear and ties.

Chiack

One is 'having a go' at one's *mate.* To indulge in a mild form of sarcasm. Normally used in the responsive or negative sense thus, "Stop chiacking me, will you, you *bloody bastard*".

Chippie
A carpenter.

Chips
Salted potato slices that come in a sealed packet – crisps or potato chips. In Australia, French fries are known as 'hot chips' – a staple of the nation's diet.

Chockers
Something that is chockers or 'chock-a-block' is full, overcrowded or replete. As well as a place being chockers, a person can be chockers with *tucker* or *grog*.

Choke a brown dog
Almost anything nasty will choke a brown dog. However, black dogs and black and white dogs seem impervious to various types of culinary poisoning. The phrase normally goes, "Jeez (a euphemism for Jesus), that pie was as *rough as guts* – it would choke a brown dog, it would". Why brown dogs in Australia are more susceptible to ptomaine poisoning than those of a different colour remains a mystery.

Chook
The common name for a chicken or, alternatively, a derogatory term for an older woman – as in "you silly old chook".

Chuck a U-ey
To make a U-turn in one's vehicle. Also 'hang a U-ey'.

Chuck a wobbly
To make a scene or throw a tantrum – also known as a 'tanty'.

Chrissie
The Australian 'baby-talk' abbreviation for Christmas. An example – "What are *youse* doin' for Chrissie?".

Chunder
A *Technicolour yawn*. To vomit or *shout for Ruth*.

Clayton's
A substitute or imitation – not the real thing. As in, "It's not for real, they're only having a Clayton's romance". Derived from a non-alcoholic drink of the same name, which was advertised as "the drink you have when you're not having a drink". Understandably, the product has never been particularly popular.

Clucky
Someone who feels the need to have children could be described as ducky, as in a broody *chook*.

Cluey
Well-informed, on the ball, and intelligent.

Coathanger, The
The Sydney Harbour Bridge.

Cobber

An archaic and now clichéd word to describe one's *mate* or true friend as in, *"G'day* cobber, let's go and have a couple of *quick snorts* for old times' sake". Dead drunk, the pair of them would go back to the motel to meet the *missus,* who by this stage was climbing the wall. In other words they were very drunk indeed and she was extremely annoyed. In the far distant past, one's cobber could be a dead crayfish on a string which one took on a tram and paid its fare. Boiled crayfish, however, were very reluctant cobbers.

Cockatoo

A large, white, sulphur-crested parrot, with a raucous voice, native to the country – the abbreviation is *cocky.* Also a lookout at an illegal gambling game who keeps an eye open for the *coppers.*

Cocky

In modern usage a farmer of any sort, social standing or wealth (*see also* BOSS COCKY). In the nineteenth and early part of this century it was a derisory term for a small landholder (50 hectares or thereabouts), who got everything wrong, was mean, and starved his workmen half to death. These days cockies remain at liberty to starve themselves but industrial law prevents them from starving the farmhands. Cocky is also an abbreviation for cockroach or *cockatoo*.

Cocky on the biscuit tin

A complicated expression which owes its origin to the rosella parrot eating a Sao cracker, as shown on tins of Arnott's biscuits. Arnotts use the rosella as a trademark. The literal translation is rhyming slang for 'on the outside looking in'. Used by members of the rank and file of any union when their elected representatives are engaged in wage discussions with the management and they haven't the slightest idea of what is going on, thus: "Out here like the *bloody* cocky on the *bloody* biscuit tin".

Cocky's cage

One is said to have 'a mouth like the bottom of a cocky's cage' when one is suffering from a terminal hangover.

Cocky's joy

Golden syrup. The only cheap sweetening available to a *cocky* or farmer in the early days of settlement because jam cost too much (even the wretched melon and lemon). Misery on a *selection* (land grant) is explained in the following saying: "The river flooded, me horse dropped dead, the damned wet dog got into me bedding and the ants got into me Cocky's Joy".

Coldie

A can or bottle of cold beer.

Colliwobbles
One can have a 'case of the colliwobbles' if one is '*crook* in the guts' – sick.

Come good
If something comes good it improves or turns out well. "She was really *crook* with the 'flu last week, but she's come good now".

Come in spinner
An expression from *two-up,* informing someone they have just been duped.

Come up smelling of roses
To extricate one's self from a difficult situation without getting into the shit. A piece of good luck.

Compo
To be 'on compo' means to be on workers' compensation; that is, receiving a temporary disability pension for injuries received at one's workplace.

Cooee
A supposed call of communication or recognition in the *bush* invented by early nineteenth century travelling journalists visiting Australia to enliven their otherwise dull copy.
See also WITHIN COOEE.

Cop this, young 'Arry
An extremely archaic phrase used by comedian Roy 'Mo' Rene when he was about to punch someone in the ear. A warning that something unpleasant is about to occur.

Copper
A policeman.

Copping it sweet

Taking things easy; having a quiet and pleasant day with a case of beer and a bag of prawns. Also, taking the blame.

Cot

Bed; not necessarily of the kiddies' variety. An example: "Did you get that *sheila* into the cot last night?"

Cot case

Describes someone who is incapacitated and should be in bed; be it due to exhaustion, stress, illness or merely intoxication.

Couldn't

The start of a number of dismissive phrases, such as 'couldn't catch a cold', 'couldn't lie straight in bed', 'couldn't train a choko vine to grow up a *dunny* wall', 'couldn't run a *chook* raffle in a country *pub*' – all of which mean that the person in question is both stupid and untrustworthy.

Country mile

An indeterminate distance, but generally one that is far longer than an actual mile. If a horse wins a race by a country mile, it has won by a considerable distance. *See also* GO FOR THE DOCTOR.

Couple of pies short of a grand final

Used to describe some one stupid or 'dense'. Similar expressions are: *brick short of a load, kangaroos in the top paddock, not the full bottle, sandwich short of a picnic* and *snag short of a barbie.*

Cow

The phrase 'a fair cow' means that things are crook – thus it can be a 'fair cow of a day'. Likewise, 'a cow of a job' means that the job is *crook*. One can also have 'a cow of a *missus*'. The amiable bovine is much maligned in the Australian language.

Cozzie

A swimming costume, as in, "Hold on a jiff until I get me cozzie on". Also known as 'swimmers', *bathers* or *togs*.

Crack hardy

To act in a courageous manner, put on a brave front, or to put up with conditions of extreme hardship when one would much prefer a glass of rum in a quiet, warm place.

Crack on to

To chat someone up, or show you have an interest in them – as in, "That *bloke*'s been trying to crack on to me all night".

Cranky

Bad-tempered, mad or both. Normally used in conjunction with *bloody* and *bastard,* thus, "He's a cranky *bloody bastard* he is".

Crawler

Someone who is *lower than a snake's belly.* A person who fawns upon a superior in the hope of obtaining present or future favours.

Creeping Jesus

(derog.) A clergyman. *See also* GOD BOTHERER.

Crook as Rookwood

Near to death; Rookwood being a vast cemetery in the city of Sydney.

Crook

In addition to the normal meaning of a dishonest person, *crook* means that one is slightly off colour, usually due to a hangover On the other hand 'crook in the guts' is the universal male expression for being genuinely sick due to an abdominal upset. To 'go crook at' or 'go crook on' means to reprimand or lose one's temper with someone.

Crooked as a dog's hind leg

Describes a person who is not to be trusted.

Crooked Mick of the Speewa

A home-grown mythical Australian *bush* hero. In keeping with Australian male tradition, Crooked Mick, apart from being able,,,, to do anything better than anyone else, was also a sometime thief, a drunkard and a liar. The Speewa itself was a mythical sheep *station* on the Murray River, although it was sometimes moved to Queensland to add authenticity to the *yarn*.

Cross, The

Kings Cross, Sydney's notorious nightlife district. This formerly colourful and truly bohemian suburb is now the dingy domain of drug addicts, strip clubs and backpackers.

Croweater

A person from South Australia.

Cruel

To spoil someone's chances or generally *bugger* things up.

Crust

One's manner of making money, hence the query, "What do you do for a crust, *mate?*"

Cut lunch

Aussie for sandwiches or a pre-packed lunch.

Dag

The wool on a sheep's rear end, usually dirty with droppings. 'Cutting out the dags' is a term used by shearers when crutching sheep at the beginning of summer to prevent flystrike. The word is also used as a term of insult as in, "He's a dag", meaning that the person is dull, boring and decidedly untrendy. In American slang, a wimp. *See also* RATTLE YOUR DAGS.

Daggy

The adjective relating to *dag*. The word can also be used affectionately to describe someone who is deeply unfashionable, but who couldn't give a *rat's arse* about it.

Dales

Trousers, particularly those worn by men. *See also* STRIDES, TRACKIE DAKS *and* UNDERDAKS.

Damper

An appalling sort of bread, devised out of sheer necessity by early white settlers and explorers, now sold at wildly inflated prices in 'Modem Australian' or *'Bush Tucker'*-style restaurants. It consists of a flour and water dough paste flung into the filthy ashes of a eucalyptus camp fire, with indescribable results. It was normally eaten with a pannikin of rum and a slice of half-bad corned beef.

Dark on

If you're dark on someone, you're angry with them.

Darlo

Darlinghurst, a not very salubrious inner-city suburb of Sydney. The hangout of drunks, trendies, *shirt-lifters, lezzos* and other colourful characters.

Darwin stubby

A very large bottle of beer – see STUBBY.

Dead Heart

The arid centre of Australia (similar to *The Red Centre),* which early explorers believed was filled with water. Many of them suffered severely for this misconception.

Dead horse

Although it's dying out now, rhyming slang was once an important component of *Aussie* speech. However, dead horse, alias 'sauce', is still used by many. Also 'rocking horse'.

Dead marine

An empty beer bottle, but definitely not an empty aluminium beer can.

Dead ringer

'He's a dead ringer for Mel Gibson' – that is, he closely resembles the famous movie star.

Dead set

A racing term meaning that the horse is an absolute or dead set certainty to win the race. The statement is invariably untrue, as is almost all racing advice. The term can also mean 'correct' or 'spot on'.

Deadhead

A deadhead is similar to a *dickhead,* but the word implies someone who is even more dull and foolish.

Delicate as a starved dingo

The person referred to has appalling table manners. "She picked at her food about as delicately as a starved dingo". The Australian native wild dog or *dingo* is not noted for its good behaviour at mealtimes.

Demo

A demonstration. *Aussies* love abbreviations.

Derro

A derelict or down-and-outer who is also probably on the *'turps'* or *'metho'*. In the good old days if the *coppers* caught the derro in a public park they would 'vag' him (that is, arrest and charge him under the Vagrancy Act as having no visible means of support). This method of getting one's arrest tallies up for the month, and thus earning promotion the easy way by persecuting the dispossessed of this earth, is now illegal in most States – much to the fury of the police.

Dickhead

A person of no consequence. A fool or a wiseguy. One's boss is invariably a dickhead.

Didn't come down in the last shower

An Australian version of the expression "I wasn't born yesterday you know". Sometimes "pull the other leg, it rings' is substituted. The remark is made after hearing a barefaced lie by one who hopes to gain a financial or other form of advantage from telling the untruth.

Digger

Initially one who took part in the gold rushes in New South Wales and Victoria in the nineteenth century. Now the term for an Australian foot soldier under the rank of corporal. This second meaning came into general currency during World War I on the redoubts of Gallipoli. At the time the members of the opposing Turkish army were at a loss to understand why Australians were willing to needlessly sacrifice their lives for perfidious Albion. These days the very few remaining survivors who march on Anzac Day (25 April) are at an equal loss. *See also* ANZAC.

Dill

A *bloody* fool.

Dillybag

From an Aboriginal source, originally meaning a grass or fibre bag used by indigenous people, but now used to describe a small bag for carrying virtually anything.

Ding dong

An impromptu and spontaneous bout of fisticuffs involving a large number of participants of either sex. Ding dongs used to be regarded in an affectionate manner but have now been replaced by the deadly serious sporting riot.

Dingbat

Someone with *kangaroos in his or her top paddock*. Crazy but not dangerously so.

Dingo

A native dog of rather clean appearance and habits (apart from at mealtimes). In human parlance, a swine or a *bastard*. In semi-jocular fashion an unexpected dinner guest, in certain strata of society, can be greeted with the remark, "Did they forget to feed the *bloody* dingoes then?"

Dingo's breakfast

A *piss,* a scratch and a good look round; in other words, none at all.

Dinki-di

True blue; on the level. The absolute truth.

Dinkum

Absolutely authentic, as in the expression, *"Fair dinkum mate,* I wouldn't lie to you, now would I?" The answer to this is, of course, "Yes".

Dip my lid

To take off one's hat to someone; a salute not necessarily to a woman out of politeness. One can dip one's lid (metaphorically speaking) to a male who has performed some generous or courageous act. The phrase is going out of fashion due to the decline in male headgear.

Dip out

To renege; to refuse to participate. Mainly used in public bars as in, "I'll dip out on this one," meaning that one does not want a drink.

Dirty

Has two meanings as in, 'I'm dirty on him,' meaning annoyed and 'Don't do the dirty on me,' meaning don't let me down or doublecross me. 'Do the dirty' often refers to a spouse who is being unfaithful.

Do a Melba

Dame Nellie Melba (1861–1931), Australia's legendary soprano, made so many farewells in her attempt to retire that this expression has passed into the language. Anyone 'doing a Melba' is therefore in the habit of making repeated returns from retirement.

Do a Harry Holt
To disappear; rhyming slang for 'to bolt'. Harold Holt was a 1960s Australian Prime Minister who vanished without a trace in the ocean off the south coast of Victoria in 1967.

Do your block
Normally preceded by the word, 'don't'. A warning to a friend or enemy not to lose one's temper or start throwing punches. The phrase, 'Don't do your 'nana', can be substituted.

Do your dash
To reach your physical limit or run out of ideas.

Dob
To incriminate someone as in, "The *bastard* dobbed me in to the *bloody coppers*". A 'dobber' is therefore an informer.

Doco
A documentary.

Dog
(derog.) An ugly woman.

Dogger
A professional *dingo* hunter who makes a living by killing wild dogs for the bounty on their scalps.

Doggo
To 'lie doggo' means that one is keeping quiet about matters and attempting to remain inconspicuous.

Dogs are barking
A hot racecourse tip as in, "Everyone know's he's got a chance, all the *bloody* dogs are barking".

Dog's breakfast/dinner

The person or object referred to is unkempt, untidy or a mess.

Dole bludger

Someone who is resting at the expense of the State due to the fact that he or she cannot find employment. Very rich people, who stand to the right of the soup spoon in Australian politics, delude themselves into believing that there is plenty of work for anyone who wants to look for it. Thus anyone who is on the dole is automatically a *bludger*.

Don, The

Sir Donald Bradman, the legendary cricketer who captained Australia from 1936–48.

Done like a dinner

To be badly beaten either in a fist fight, a business deal, or at sport. A horse that loses a race can also be done like a dinner.

Donger

The penis.

Doover

Anything that one cannot get hold of one's self while the tractor, car or washing machine is blowing up. Thus, "For Christ's sake hand me that doover will *youse?*"
The recipient of this information will invariably hand the person in question the wrong doover and the tractor will explode. Also called 'dooverlackie'. International translations are 'doodad' and 'thingummyjig'.

Dose

Short form of 'dose of the shits'. Normally applied to a person that one dislikes, thus, "He gives me a dose".

Down the drain

Things have turned out for the worse. The horse has lost the race and therefore one's money is down the drain. Sometimes expressed as 'down the gurgler', which is a drain by another name.

Down the hatch

An expression uttered before taking a beer with a *mate*. The expression, *here's looking at you sideways* is equally appropriate and proper on these social occasions because when drinking, one does normally have to observe one's friend in this fashion.

Down Under

Australia – also known as *Godzone, Oz, The Lucky Country, Striya* and *The Sunburnt Country*.

Drack

Dowdy or slovenly in one's personal attire.

Drag the chain

A person is said to be dragging the chain if he is either loafing on the job or not drinking fast enough. To loaf on the job is acceptable but to fall behind in a drinking *school* is regarded as a crime.

Draining the dragon

The act of (male) urination, or 'shaking hands with the unemployed'. *See also* POINTING PERCY AT THE PORCELAIN.

Dreg

An unkempt person of either sex; someone who is both boring and not upwardly mobile. The word is much used by females in reference to a male, who, in international terms, can be described as an arsehole.

Drink with the flies

A person who is an outcast of society, or otherwise disliked by society, is said to drink with the flies because they are his only companions.

Drongo

A stupid person; an idiot. Similar to a *deadhead*.

Droob

A fool.

Dropkick

A method of scoring points in rugby and *Aussie Rules*. Also someone despicable – see REAL DROPKICK.

Dropped his bundle

Basically literary reference to throwing one's *swag* into the bushes, giving one's dog to the local butcher and then hanging one's self from the handy beam of a nearby shanty (after carefully removing one's boots). In short, to give up and admit failure in this vale of tears which some people call life.

Drover's dog

An inoffensive animal that for many years went about its job quietly – which, basically, was ankle-tapping cattle. Then in the early 1980s it learned, to its own intense surprise, that it was capable of winning elections and governing the country. Despite the fact that this lowered its social status, the dog *showed willing* and governed Australia in a capable fashion.

Drum, the

The *good oil;* the truth.

Dry as an old lady's talcum powder

The feminist version of an offensive phrase used by males, 'dry as a nun's nasty'. The bisexual phrases are 'dry as a dead *dingo's donger'*, 'dry as a *Pam's* towel' and 'dry as a *drover's dog'*. All of these expressions mean that the person in question is in desperate need of an alcoholic drink.

Dry blanket

A hot afternoon or day hence, "It's like a *bloody* dry blanket in here today".

Dry, The

The dry season, experienced in tropical northern Australia, generally between the months of May and November. *See also* WET, THE.

Dubbo

A slow-witted, but relatively harmless, country person, similar to a *bushie.* From the name of an exciting inland town in New South Wales.

Duckshove

To avoid responsibility; to push an unpleasant task into the lap of another.

Duds

Male clothing, as in, "Get your duds on and we'll go out and get on the *piss* and pick up a couple of *sheilas*". Females don't wear duds, they are clothed either in frocks or outfits.

Duff

If one duffs cattle one steals them. If a woman is *up the duff* she is pregnant. But if one is a duffer one is a *bloody* fool. The word defies further analysis.

Dull as dishwater

The person being spoken of, is.

Dumper

A large wave that picks up a body surfer and slams him into the bottom of the beach, causing joy to the medical profession and terror to his medical insurance company.

Dunderhead

A fool.

Dungaree settler

Archaic. An early member of the blue jeans set who settled in the Hawkesbury River area of the infant colony of New South Wales. Most were poor and the survivors quickly became inbred. In short, a term of derision similar to the Americanism 'cracker white'.

Dunny

An outside lavatory or 'bog' which has given rise to the following famous jingle:

> Don't sit upon
> The dunny seat
> The crabs in here
> Can jump six feet.

This is a non-metricated version of the fact that lavatory seats in public toilets are infested with the whimsical and amusing crab louse. 'Dunnican' was a pan removed once a week by a specially trained 'dunnican man' in the dead of night in non-sewered metropolitan areas. Apart from his wages, his annual reward was either half a crown or a case of beer at Christmas.

Dunny-diver

An imaginative name for a plumber.

Durry

A cigarette.

Ear basher
A *pub* bore.

Eat the horse, chase the rider
An expression shouted by a disappointed *punter* after his selection has *dipped out* or 'run out of the money'. He or she has 'done the rent' which will inevitably lead to a 'domestic' (punch up with one's spouse) later on in the day.

Enzed
From NZ, the acronym for New Zealand. *See also* KIWI LAND.

Esky
A portable icebox that can be filled with grog, *tucker* and ice – the essential *Aussie* summer accessory. Known, strangely, as a 'chillybin' in *Kiwi Land*.

Face fungus
A beard, moustache, or other form of facial hair.

Face like a stopped clock
The person being referred to is either ugly, or stunned, or both.

Fair crack of the whip
Someone is not giving the utterer of the phrase a *fair* go, probably by drinking too fast or stealing the cocaine, thus the expression (uttered in outrage), "Fair crack of the whip, *mate*". *See also* FAIR SUCK OF THE SAUCE BOTTLE.

Fair dinkum
The absolute truth as in, "He's a fair dinkum *bastard,* fair dinkum he is, he's fair dinkum, my *bloody oath*". As a general observation anyone who utters such a phrase can be regarded as, 'three sheets to the wind', 'pissed as a parrot', or just drunk.

Fair go
Said by someone who is asking for a *fair crack of the whip.*

Fair suck of the sauce bottle
Another person who is not getting a *fair crack of the whip.* An alternative is 'fair suck of the *sav'.*

Fart in a bottle
Someone is 'behaving like a ...'. Farts are believed to behave somewhat oddly when contained in bottles.

Feather duster

A descriptive term, normally confined to the future of politicians as in, "This week he's top rooster but next week he'll be nothing but a *bloody* feather duster". Although feather dusters have been made almost obsolete due to the invention of the vacuum cleaner, the expression persists.

Feeding time at the zoo

Similar expression to 'shark feeding frenzy'. A scene of uncoordinated lunacy involving a large number of people. The behaviour of a group of Australians at a buffet table; bedlam and greed combined.

Fella

A man or fellow. The word is used frequently by Aboriginal people.

First cab off the rank

The person who is entitled to his or her reward because he or she is at the head of the queue. Sometimes this means that the person in question is the first to be sacked or shot. It has some similarity with the phrase, 'first in, best dressed'.

Fit as a Mallee bull

Used to describe someone who is fighting fit and in excellent health: 'strong as a Mallee bull' is a variation. *See also* MALLEE, THE.

Fizzer

'The party was a real fizzer' – a dismal failure.

Flake

Shark meat, often sold by fishmongers as the 'fish' in fish and chips.

Flash as a rat with a gold tooth
A person who is ostentatious, over-dressed and generally tasteless.

Flat chat
To move or travel at high speed; 'flat tack' has the same meaning. *See also* FULL BORE.

Flat out like a lizard drinking
Similar to *flat chat,* but more appropriate for someone who is working hard or at speed.

Flick
A rejection or the big brush-off. Someone who has been sacked from their job might be asked: "Did they give you the flick?". A girl who's just told her boyfriend where to go could say: "I gave that *drongo* the flick last night".

Flicks, the
The cinema, as in, "Let's go to the flicks tonight".

Floater
A meat pie which has been placed in a soup bowl full of mashed, dried, blue boiler peas and then topped with *dead horse.* A favourite dish of people who live in the city of Adelaide, it has failed to rate a mention in *Larousse Gastronomique.*

Floating on ice
Drunk.

Fly bog
Somewhat archaic now, but a colourful name for jam.

Footie/Footy

Abbreviations for football, the various forms of which are a national obsession. *Aussie Rules* is played primarily in Victoria, South Australia, Western Australia, Tasmania and the Northern Territory; Rugby League (also known simply as *League)* and Rugby Union in New South Wales, the Australian Capital Territory and southern Queensland; while soccer is played mostly by *Poms,* by people of European and South American descent, and by other *New Australians.* The word also applies to the ball – be it round or oval.

Footpath

The Australian version of pavement, sidewalk, etc.

Form

In reference to racehorses, if the four-footed idiot has 'good form' it may well win the race. If a human being is in 'good form' it means that he or she is being witty and entertaining.

Fossick

To search for gold where others have failed to find it. To 'fossick around', however, simply means to search for something.

Four b' two

An unmetricated piece of timber which is widely used throughout the country to hammer sense into the skulls of dumb animals. Politicians are widely threatened with this treatment as in, "You'd have to take a piece of four b' two to the *bastard* to make him see the sense of it". An implement of discipline; a pick handle in the rough.

Fourpenny dark

An archaic word for cheap red fortified wine, similar to *plank* and usually quite nasty.

Freo

The port of Fremantle, in Western Australia.

Full as a

The start of many expressions; 'full as a butcher's pup',
'full as a goog' and 'full as a State school' to name but three.
All refer to the fact that the speaker is 'as *pissed as a parrot*'.
Intoxicated.

Full bore

To go all out, to give one's best as in, "He came at me full
bore but I *stoushed* the *bastard* anyway".

Furphy

An Australian-Irish expression meaning a lie, as in, "That's
a *bloody* furphy, *mate*". Singular only. No-one in his or her
right mind attempts to put over a bunch of furphies.

G

G, The
The vast (it seats around 100,000 people) MCG, or
Melbourne Cricket Ground – the main stadium for the
1956 Olympic Games, and a legendary cricket and *Aussie
Rules* venue.

Gabba, The
Brisbane's premier cricket ground, located in the improbably
named suburb of Woolloongabba.

Galah
One of the more beautiful birds of Australia's dry areas with
its rose-coloured breast, its impressive crests and its pink-
grey wings. In flight a flock of galahs, although raucous, is
sheer poetry. In human parlance, a *bloody* fool. *See also*
MAD AS A GUMTREE FULL OF GALAHS.

Garbo
A garbage or rubbish collector, referred to in polite society
as a 'garbologist'.

G'day
Good day – the universal *Aussie* greeting, pronounced
'g-deh' rather than 'g-die'.

Gee up
To gee up your *footie* team is to *barrack* for them, thereby
encouraging them and lifting their spirits.

Geek

A look – as in, "Give us a geek at the newspaper" or "Have a geek at this". Similar to a *squiz*.

Get a bag

Now rarely used, but once a popular cricketing term of abuse uttered by those sitting in the cheap seats. Means that the fielder to whom the abuse is directed has dropped an easy catch.

Get nicked

See NICK OFF.

Get stuck into

A phrase meant to encourage one's *mates* to work hard, thus, "If we get stuck into this lot right away we'll be down at the *boozer* in no time at all". Also, to abuse someone verbally or physically.

Getting off at Redfern

Although little used nowadays, this was once a very popular euphemism for *coitus interruptus*. Redfern is the last station before Sydney's Central railway terminus.

Gibber

A stone or a small rock. Australia is famous in geological circles for its stony or gibber deserts. European beaches are, to the astonishment of most Australians, mainly composed of gibbers.

Gin

(derog.) An archaic term for a female Aborigine, also known as a *lubra*.

Give it a burl

To give something a burl is to *give it a* go – see below. *Go for a burl,* however, is somewhat different.

Give it a go

A term of encouragement, sometimes translated as *give it a burl*. Similar to *get stuck into*, meaning once again that as soon as we all get together and get this job over and done with the quicker we can get to the *boozer*.

Give it a miss

Means that one is about to *dip out*, as in, "Well I wouldn't mind going to the races with you but I'll cop it from the missus and so I think I'll give it a miss this time. But I'll catch up with *youse* later".

Go bush

See BUSH.

Go crook

See CROOK.

Go for a burl

To take the family car out illegally for a high speed run involving the forces of law and order at some stage. After one has been for a *burl* one's father 'beats the shit' out of one.

Go for the doctor

A racing term. If a horse has gone for the doctor it is about to win the race by a *country mile*.

Go for your life

An encouragement to participate whole heartedly – as in, "Hey Gazza [that is, 'Gary'], can I open another bottle of grog?" "*Shit-yeh*, go for your life!" 'Go for it' is a variation.

Go under (someone's) neck

To take unfair advantage, thus, "I thought I had the job but the *bloody bastard* went under me neck".

Go walkabout

See WALKABOUT.

Goanna oil

A mythical oil made from the flesh of boiled down lizards (goannas) who were doing no-one any harm until the arrival of Europeans in the continent. It has the reputation of being able to eat its way through glass containers as well as being able to cure cancer. Entirely different from the *good oil,* which is spot-on information, as in a hot racing tip. Both oils are a load of rubbish.

God botherer

(derog.) A man of the cloth. A clergyman of the Christian persuasion. *See also* CREEPING JESUS.

Godzone

A succinct adaptation of 'God's Own Country' Australia.

Gone to the pack

Someone who has failed.

Gong, a

An award or medal.

Gong, The

Not to be confused with *a gong,* this term refers to the New South Wales city of Wollongong.

Good-oh!

An expression of delight or agreement. 'Good one' is similar, but less emphatic.

Good oil

The truth; correct information. Similar to *the drum.*

Good on ya!

Used to express approval and even admiration: the *Aussie* equivalent of the much more restrained British term 'Good for you'. The phrase is usually finished – at least by males – with the word *mate*. *See also* ONYA!

Good sort

A grouse-looking *sheila*.

Goog

An egg. 'Googy-egg' is also used.

Got the game by the throat

In control of a given situation, as in, "*No worries, missus,* the verandah'll be finished by tomorrow, we've got the game by the throat".

Great Australian salute

A tongue-in-cheek description of the *Aussie* practice of waving one's arms and hands around the head and neck to discourage flies and other airborne pests.

Greenie

A rabid left-wing member of the alternative society who, although violently opposed to the destruction of forests, expects to get both his milk and his newspaper delivered daily.

Grey ghost

An inspector of parking meters – derived from the colour of the uniform. 'Grey meanie' and 'brown bomber' are both alternatives.

Grizzle

To constantly complain and *whinge*. One who grizzles could be described as a 'grizzleguts'.

Grog

Alcohol of virtually any variety (as opposed to *plank*): also known, in less polite circles, as booze or *piss*. To 'grog on' means to become involved in a major drinking session – to 'hit the *piss*' or 'get on the *piss*'.

Grommet

A term from the surfing world, meaning a young (generally teenage) *surfie*.

Grouse

Good. One can have a 'grouse feed' or a 'grouse time'. A *sheila* can be grouse but a *bloke* never is.

Guernsey

If one 'gets a guernsey' or is given one, one is deemed to have succeeded in one's given task.

Gutful

A gutful is more than enough – as in, "I've had a gutful of that *bloody sheila*".

Had the claw

Something or someone is *buggered*. Normally used in reference to a piece of machinery which will no longer work as in, "Sorry, *mate,* but your washing machine's had the *bloody* claw". Pieces of machinery can also be deemed to have 'had the sword', 'had the Richard' or 'had the Dick'.

Happy as a bastard on Father's Day
Extremely unhappy.

Happy as Larry
Extremely happy, although God alone knows why the Larrys of this world should be in a continuous state of merriment. 'Happy as a pig in shit' is an alternative expression.

Hard word

If one puts the hard word on a *sheila* one expects her to 'come across' – to have sexual intercourse. If one puts the hard word on one's *mate* one expects at least a tenner ($10).

Hatter

A solitary bushman, usually half mad. Although derived from the English phrase, 'as mad as a hatter' (because they were made mad by the use of mercury in the hat-making business), it has absolutely nothing to do with headgear.

Have a shot at

To a tempt to take the *piss* out of someone else verbally as in, "The *bastard* had a shot at me but I told him where he could get off. The *bastard* can go to *buggery* as far as I am concerned".

Hawkesbury duck

An archaic expression for an ear of maize or a corncob with the kernels intact. Road gang convicts used to steal these cobs from nearby farmers' fields when they thought they would not be detected. A derisory phrase meaning that one has very little to eat. Still used occasionally in the *bush* to give vent to the feelings that one is hard up through no fault of one's own. So if one is making one's dinner from Hawkesbury duck there is 'not a *skerrick* left' in the house.

Hay, Hell and Booligal

The nasty end of *Woop Woop*. Nowhere, or the fag end of the universe, or as our great *Aussie* poet Banjo Paterson put it, "the infernal regions of heat, dust and flies". Normally uttered thus: "I'm *buggered* if I know where he's gone, it's all Hay, Hell and Booligal here, *mate*". In the literal sense the township of Hungerford on the New South Wales–Queensland border, being somewhat *Back o' Bourke,* is Hay, Hell and Booligal to a T.

Haybumer

A horse.

Headless chook

See LIKE A BLUE-ARSED FLY.

Heart-starter

An alcoholic drink, particularly one taken early in the day, often in a vain attempt to cure last night's hangover.

Hen's teeth

As scarce as. Even *Blind Freddy* knows that hens have no teeth. *See also* ROCKING HORSE SHIT.

Here's looking at you sideways

A verbal thank-you to a *mate* who has just shouted you to a *schooner.*

He's got a head on him like a robber's dog
He's as 'ugly as a hatful of arseholes'.

High as a dingo's howl
Used to describe something that smells appalling or *on the nose*.

Hit the frog and toad
Rhyming slang for 'hit the road'.

Hit the kapok
To state one's intention of going to bed to sleep. One can also state that one is going to 'Bungidoo', 'snatch a stretch of shut eye', 'somolosa', 'hit the *cot'*, or express the intention of being about to be 'wrapped in the arms of Murphys'. For the sub-literate, Murphys is the Australianism of Morpheus.

Hit the nail on the head
To get to the nub of the matter.

Home and hosed
The racehorse or *hayburner* concerned has well and truly *gone for the doctor*. In political terms, "The polls are closed and your loyal supporters are *pissing* it up in your opponent's office". Someone has won something.

Hoon
A high-class *dole bludger*. An idiot. Also, someone who likes to drive fast and loud, and generally make mischief in the street. Is also used as a verb – to 'hoon' around town.

Hoop
A jockey.

Hooroo/Ooroo
Literally goodbye, as in, "Well hooroo then, I'll catch yer later".

Hospital pass

A *footie* (particularly rugby) term, describing a pass that puts the recipient of the ball into an impending collision or other dangerous situation.

Howzat!

A cry made to a cricket umpire by a fielding side, as an peal to have a batsman declared out for various incomprehensible reasons. A bastardisation of 'How's that?', 'Howzat!' is normally screamed dramatically by an expectantly crouched bowler.

Hughie

God. Always used in, "Send 'er down, Hughie". Meaning, 'please God make it rain a lot'. Why the Australian God should be called Hughie, rather than the Lord of Prophets or even Father Divine, has managed to exercise the minds of psychiatrists for some little time.

Humdinger

A 'little beauty'. Something very good or excellent, as in, "You little *bloody* humdinger you, *my oath*".

Hump the bluey

To carry the *swag*.

Humpy

A bark hut.

Hungry bastard

Someone who will stop at nothing to get an extra *quid* (dollar). Someone who would steal the stamp money from his blind mother. A *shithead*.

Icky
Either a difficult or troublesome situation – "I was in a bit of an icky spot' – or just something gooey or sticky.

If it was raining palaces I'd get hit by the dunny door
One of a number of phrases meaning that one's never ever had a lucky streak or won a lottery.

Illywhacker
A *smart-arsed* trickster.

In like Flynn
One is on to a sure thing. Refers to the late Hollywood film star Errol Flynn (a Tasmanian) who, it was claimed, had his way with any woman of his choice.

Interstate
Anywhere in Australia other than one's home state – as in, "They went interstate yesterday' or "I'll be interstate for the next week".

Isa, The
Mount Isa, a bleak and rugged mining city in *Outback* Queensland and no place for the faint-hearted.

J

Jack of
To be jack of something is to be tired of, or fed up with it: "I'm jack of this *bloody* job".

Jackaroo
A generally young apprentice worker on a sheep or cattle *station*. The female equivalent is a 'jillaroo'.

Joey
A cute baby kangaroo or wallaby, usually seen in its mother's pouch.

Joe Blow
"He's just an average Joe Blow", an ordinary *bloke*.

Journo
A journalist.

Jumbuck
An archaic name for a sheep, usually a ram.

Jump the rattler
To catch an illegal ride on a train, normally by hiding in an empty wheat car.

Kacky hander

One who writes and does everything else with his or her left hand. Otherwise an awkward *bastard,* who could be said to be 'kackhanded'.

Kangaroos in the top paddock

One of many Australian phrases indicating that someone is stark, raving mad. However, the person is a harmless madman. The person concerned can also be *'a sandwich short of a picnic', 'not the full bottle',* or *'a couple of pies short of a grand final'.*

Kelpie

An Australian sheepdog breed, developed from the Scottish collie. The *blue heeler* is another famous *Aussie* working dog. *See also* BLACK BASTARD.

Kick on

To continue drinking after someone has 'found the necessary' or 'got the readies', meaning that one in the party has found enough money to buy the next round of drinks. In its more general sense, kick on means to continue partying or just having a good time.

Kick the bucket

To die.

Kick the tin

To donate to a worthy cause, especially to the widow of someone who has just *kicked the bucket*.

Killer

A bullock or sheep that has been reserved for eventual consumption on the homestead or *station* in the form of a *baked dinner*. The word can also be used, however, to mean 'effective' – as in, "That was a killer joke".

King hit

To knock someone down unfairly with a single blow, norm ally delivered without warning. If one has been king hit one has been knocked senseless. One can also be 'kinged', which is the same thing.

Kiwi Land

New Zealand: the land of both Kiwis (the people) and the kiwi (an indigenous flightless bird). *See also* ENZED.

Knock back

To be rejected (normally by a woman) as in, "I put the *hard word* on her but she knocked me back".

Knocker

One who knocks. A critic as in, "Every time I come up with a good idea the *bastard* knocks it".

Knockers

The mammary glands of a human female; tits.

Knuckle down

One who is prepared to *show willing*. If someone knuckles down to a job, he or she is deemed to be a good worker.

Knuckle sandwich

A 'bunch of fives' (a punch) delivered in the direction of one's teeth. If one 'wears a knuckle sandwich', one is not happy.

Koori

An Aborigine, and along with alternatives such as *Murri* nowadays commonly used. Also spelt 'Koorie'.

L

Lady's Waist

The subject of Australian beer measures can be very confusing, so this is the first of many entries relating to this import ant topic. A Lady's Waist used to be either a 5- or 7-ounce measure of beer once served only in the parlour of a *pub* in New South Wales, but in Queensland it was known as a 'glass' because it was taken as a chaser to a glass or shot of neat rum. In New South Wales a *schooner* is somewhat short of a pint. A pint is known as a *pot* in Victoria. In New South Wales a pint is a pint, but never has been sold as such because there were no glasses to hold that measure. A *pot* used to be a 7-ounce in Western Australia, where a *schooner* was 10 ounces, but in South Australia if you wanted a Coopers you had to ask for a bottle because only West End was sold in glasses or off the tap. In Tasmania a glass of Cascade is sold as a 'glass', while in Queensland XXXX comes in *stubbies* or *tinnies*. Other glasses include a *middy* and a *pony,* while bottled and/or canned beer comes in various sizes – including a *longnech, stubby, throwdown* and *tinny* (also known as a 'tube'). Just ask for a beer.

Lair

A flash *bastard* who plays up like *billy-o* and dresses up like a *pox doctor's clerk*. Normally anyone who is a lair is called a *'mug lair'*. A show-off. The Americanism is 'asshole'.

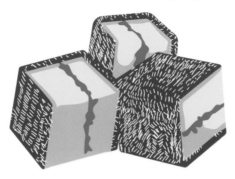

Lamington

A highly overrated but greatly revered *Aussie* confection, consisting of a square of sponge cake covered with chocolate icing and shreds of coconut.

Larrikin

A poorly dressed *mug lair* who is prone to punch-ups at the drop of a hat.

League

Short form of Rugby League – see FOOTIE.

Leave for dead

To overtake, outperform, outrun, etc. – as in, "Johnno left them for dead in the 100-metre sprint".

Leave you short

Invariably a question asked by a *cadger* or *bot* who has just borrowed money. In a vague attempt to ease his conscience after he has grabbed the rent money he asks, "Now are you sure that this won't leave you short?" It will.

Leg it

To walk: "We missed the bus and had to leg it". Or, as a command, to get the hell out of here.

Lezzo

(derog.) A lesbian.

Lick you to death

Derisory term for a watchdog that isn't. A failed *blue heeler*. The dog in question will.

Lie doggo

To keep one's head down while the shit is hitting the fan. To be extremely quiet.

Life wasn't meant to be easy

A phrase erroneously attributed to a conservative prime minister of the 1970s, meaning that one was supposed to work for one's keep.

Like a blue-arsed fly

The expressions 'Buzz around like a blue-arsed fly' and 'Run around like a *headless chook*' mean much the same – a bit like *'flat out like a lizard drinking',* but implying even more disorganisation and frantic movement.

Like a shag on a rock

Used to describe someone or something that looks lonely and forlorn. This type of shag (a bird) is definitely not to be confused with the verb, to *shag*.

Like flies around a cow yard

A rude but appropriate phrase to describe Australian *journos* clustering around a free drinks table.

Lingo

Language – as in, *"Youse* had better learn the lingo if yer goin' to France for yer holidays".

Liquid laugh

Yet another colourful expression to describe the act of vomiting. *See also* CHUNDER *and* TECHNICOLOUR YAWN.

Liquid lunch

A lunch consisting entirely of alcohol, particularly beer. *See also* TEN-OUNCE SANDWICH.

Little Aussie battler

See BATTLER.

Little green suitcase

A cask of wine. *See also* CASK.

Little Vegemite

A child, especially one who is contented and well-behaved. Derived from an advertising jingle that was long used to promote the popular product known as *Vegemite.*

Living daylights

If one has the living daylights scared out of one, one is very scared indeed.

Loaded

This can describe a person who is very wealthy, but it can also mean to be drunk.

Lob

To lob is to arrive or depart, generally unexpectedly. Someone can 'lob up' or 'lob in' (turn up unannounced, and generally hang around), or even 'lob off' (leave).

Lollies

Confectionery or sweets, particularly the boiled variety. Known as 'candy' in North America and 'sweets' in the UK.

Lollywater

A soft drink that's so sweet it tastes like *lollies*.

Long streak of cocky's shit

Describes someone very tall and very arrogant. The phrase 'long streak of pelican's shit' means the same thing. Normally uttered by short people who feel inferior.

Longneck

A large beer bottle, containing 750 ml of *amber fluid*.

Loo, The

No, not the toilet, but an abbreviation of the improbable 'Woolloomooloo', a Sydney suburb. The name is believed to be Aboriginal for 'a young kangaroo'.

Lord Muck

An expression of abuse as in '*bloody* Lord Muck of Shit Hall'. The person uttering the phrase is in effect stating that some one has risen above his or her station in life and has adopted the affectations of the English nobility. But he or she has *buggered* it up and cannot understand the use of snail tongs let alone the *doover* for asparagus. A *mug lair* in fancy dress and language.

Lousy

One is '*crook* in the guts' or otherwise off-colour.

Lower than a snake's belly
Describes a *dead set bastard*.

Lubra
(derog.) A female Aborigine, also once known as a *gin*.

Lucky Country, The
Australia. Although originally an ironic term, coined by
writer Donald Home in the 1960s, the expression now
implies that Australia is *the* land of good fortune. *See also*
DOWN UNDER, GODZONE, OZ and STRIYA.

Lunatic soup
Alcohol in any form. Normally uttered by a police
spokesman as in, "Well, we could contain them until the
bastards really got stuck into the lunatic soup".

Lurk
One can lurk, as in hide or hang around in a furtive manner,
but a lurk is also an easy or favourable situation – as in,
"Shazza's [that is, 'Sharon's] new job is a bit of a lurk".

Mad as a cut snake

Both crazy and angry. Any Australian snake which has been cut in half doesn't take kindly to its aggressor. 'Mad as a meat axe' is a similar expression.

Mad as a gumtree full of galahs

Similar to *mad as a cut snake,* but implying plain insanity rather than being angry as well as mad. *See* GALAH.

Madwoman's breakfast/knitting/lunch

In a dreadful mess. Mad women are deemed to be somewhat sloppy by the general populace.

Mag

A talk, or to talk to another, as in, "We had a good mag". Also known as a 'chinwag'.

Makings

If one asks for the makings one expects to receive in return a packet of fine-cut tobacco, cigarette papers and a box of matches, hence the query, "You wouldn't have the makings about you, *mate,* would you?"

Mallee, The

An Aboriginal word meaning a low-growing but extremely hardy tree species. The Mallee, therefore, is a region generally hot, dry remote and bleak – which features this type of vegetation. *See also* FIT AS A MALLEE BULL.

Manchester
An archaic term that originated in England (but which is practically never used there nowadays) to describe sheets, towels and other household linen.

Map of Tassie
The female pubic hair area, the shape of which resembles the roughly triangular outline of the island of Tasmania.

Marvel
As in the statement, "You're a *bloody* marvel; I hope they can breed off you". A sarcastic remark directed at someone who has *buggered* things up.

Mate
In most English-speaking countries a 'mate' is someone or something that people and animals mate with. In Australia, how ever, 'mate' is what men (and a small proportion of women) call their friends, buddies or pals. The word is also part of a universal greeting among *Aussie* males – as in, 'How ya goin' mate?", addressed to everyone from the best friend to someone you've never laid eyes on before. If one is being particularly affectionate, 'matey' is permissible. However, 'mate' can also be used aggressively, as in, "What are you looking at, mate?" – meaning, "keep looking at me and I'll *king hit* you".

Mateship

An *Aussie* male condition – the state of being *mates* with just about every other Australian *bloke*.

Mate's rates

Special reduced rates or fees for one's *mates*.

Matilda

An assortment of one's personal possessions rolled up in a blanket – a *swag*. If one goes *'waltzing Matilda'*, in the words of the national song, one is deemed to be *'humping the bluey on the wallaby'*.

Met fairy

A meteorologist, because they're always playing with balloons.

Metho

A drinker of methylated spirits, or just the product itself often consumed in refined circles with a dash of fruit cordial to cut the taste. A metho is generally also a *derro*.

Mexican

A New South Wales term, used to describe those from south of the border (Victorians).

Mick

A Roman Catholic, particularly one of Irish extraction. *See also* TYKE.

Middy

A medium-size beer glass; similar to a *pot,* but smaller than a *schooner. See also* LADY'S WAIST.

Miserable as a bandicoot

Extremely unhappy. A bandicoot is a small furry marsupial undeserving of this association.

Missus, the
The wife, the 'little woman'.

Mob
A large number of people, kangaroos, sheep, or other
animals. The word can also be used to refer to one's friends
and family, as in "We had the mob over for *tea* last night".
The word is particularly well-used by *Koori* people.

Mongrel
As well as referring to a dog of mixed origins (*see* BITZER),
mongrel can describe something or someone that is
particularly unpleasant, difficult, or badly behaved – "Being
a *garbo* is a mongrel of a job", or "Behave yourself, you *bloody*
mongrel".

More front than Myers
Used to describe someone who is exceptionally cheeky or
self-assured. Myers is a chain of department stores, housed in
large buildings with big windows. An alternative is 'more
front than Grace Brothers'.

More-ish

Something or someone delicious, particularly food, that you just can't get enough of – chocolate, cake, biscuits, for example. A *bloke* who has just started going out with a *good sort* might describe her as very more-ish.

Motza

If one scores a motza one has won a packet. To win the lottery or otherwise be in luck.

Mozzy

The plural of the word is 'mozzies' – that is, mosquitoes, which are rumoured to be as big as pigs, with tusks as well.

Muddie

Short for Queensland mud crab, the tastiest crab along Australia's shores. Anything of the crustacean variety that is not a muddie is regarded as being 'good only for shark bait'.

Mug

Fool, loser. Often heard in the expression, "'*Ave a* go, ya mug!' when someone, usually a sportsperson, is *bludging* instead of putting some effort into it.

Mug lair

See LAIR.

Mulga

If one is 'in the mulga' one is in a particularly obnoxious part of the Australian *Outback* where the beer is warm. The scrub.

Mullock

To 'poke mullock' means to 'poke *borah*'. To insult. One can also be 'in the mullock', which is the same as being in the shit.

Mullygrubber

A low and unfair ball bowled underarm in cricket.

Murri

An indigenous Australian. *See also* KOORI.

Muso

Aussie abbreviation for a musician.

My oath

A reply to almost anything as in, "It's a hot day". "My oath". "It's a cold day". "My oath". "Would you like a drink?" "My oath". "How's about going up *The Cross* and getting on the *piss* and picking up a couple *sheilas?*" "My *bloody* oath". The phrase used to be known as 'my colonial oath' but since Federation the word 'colonial' has been dropped.

Mystery bag

Rhyming slang for a *snag*. Very appropriate when one considers the dubious nature of the contents of most sausages.

N

Nark

A *wet blanket*. Someone who *knocks* or criticises as in, "He's nothing but a *bloody* nark". In a secondary sense it means one who criticises but won't lend a hand to put things to rights.

Nasho

One who in past years was forced to serve his country for his country's good. Short for National Serviceman.

Ned Kelly

Australia's most famous bushranger, Ned was from poor Irish stock and lived in central Victoria in the 1860s–1870s. Like Robin Hood, he stole from the English landed gentry and gave to the poor. Ned's one mistake was to make a mere half suit of armour, thus allowing the *coppers* to shoot and capture him. He was then hanged. Before dying he did *not* utter the words, "Such, such is life'; a reporter from the Melbourne *Age* newspaper did. Because of this misguided dottiness Ned Kelly has become Australia's folk hero, giving rise to the phrase, *'as game as Ned Kelly'*. The variant of the phrase is 'as game as Phar Lap'. Phar Lap was a horse.

Never Never

Home of the *Outback* Aborigines, meaning the desert regions of Australia. A somewhat affectionate term for the country that is deemed to be 'beyond the *Black Stump*'. The term is also used to describe the hire-purchase or credit system.

New Australian

A polite term for a migrant, particularly someone of a non-English speaking background.

Nick off

To depart – either as in "I'd better nick off, then", or in the form of an angry instruction, similar to '*bugger* off', '*piss* off' or '*rack off*'. *Get nicked* is an alternative for the latter form.

Nipper

Either a small freshwater crustacean or a boy above the *rug rat* stage who *shows willing*.

No bloody picnic

One has emerged from a situation of almost total disaster but one is not about to admit it. Thus in reply to the question, "How'd it go then?", the correct Australian male answer is, "Well, it was no bloody picnic".

No hoper

A fool.

No worries

A terrifying phrase meaning usually that the house is going to fall down, as in "No worries, *missus, she's sweet*". Having said this the builder departs and the house does indeed fall down. A variation is 'No wuckin' furries', sometimes shortened to 'No wuckers'.

Nong

An idiot or fool.

Not half bad

Extra *grouse*. Thus the correct reply to the question as to whether one likes the vintage champagne, is, "Well, it's not half bad". This means that the product in question is excellent.

Not the full bottle

Means that someone is 'not the full *quid*' (archaic) or 'has *kangaroos in his or her top paddock*'. One of a number of phrases meaning that the person in question is 'a *brick short of a load*' or that 'You can knock but no-one answers'.

O

Ocker
The average Australian male, usually called Norm or Bruce. His going-out rig consists of a T-shirt, shorts, *thongs* and an *esky* full of *tinnies*.

Off his (or her) face
Mad or just extremely inebriated.

Off like a bride's nightie
To depart quickly. "Up and down like a bride's nightie", however, describes something that fluctuates with regularity.

Off like a bucket of prawns
Similar to *off like a bride's nightie*.

Off the hook
Safe. If one has managed to get one's self off the hook one has managed to avoid a difficult situation which means that usually one has told a barefaced lie.

Oldie
A word used by one under the age of 17 for anyone over the age of 20.

On for young and old
Something – perhaps a full-on verbal or physical brawl – in which everyone participates enthusiastically. *See also* OPEN SLATHER.

On the blink
If something is 'on the blink' it is not working properly.

On the nose
Off; literally bad smelling. Usually used in reference to a shady deal which is held to be on the nose.

On the outer
If one is 'on the outer' one is normally forced to *drink with the flies*. A position of being a temporary outcast.

On the piss/turps
To indulge excessively in alcohol.

On the wallaby
See WALLABY TRACK.

One-eyed trouser snake
The penis. A bit of a cliché that is rarely used now; one of the many creations of Barry Humphries, aka Sir Les Patterson.

Onya!
Similar to *good on ya!*, but more often shouted as a form of encouragement, especially at the *footie* and other sporting events.

Open slather
A situation or event with few, or no, restraints. Similar to *on for young and old*.

O.S.
Overseas – essentially anywhere but Australia.

Outback, The
Australia's remote, sparsely populated and generally arid regions come under this collective term, which literally means 'out the back', or beyond civilisation. Similar to the *bush,* but it implies somewhere even more inhospitable.

Over the odds

A 'bit rough'. Normally said of one who is deemed to be 'coming on *a bit strong*'. A statement that is a palpable lie.

Oz

Australia. *See also* DOWN UNDER, GODZONE, THE LUCKY COUNTRY, STRIYA, THE SUNBURNT COUNTRY.

Paddo
Paddington, a fashionable Sydney suburb.

Pass muster
To be acceptable. Anyone who passes muster can from that time on be regarded as a good *bloke*.

Pass over the Great Divide
To die or expire.

Pav
A pavlova, the famous, sweet meringue-based dessert with obscure origins, possibly invented by an Australian chef in 1935.

Pearler
Something *beaut* or very good. Can also be spelt 'purler'.

Perve
In its most general sense, the male habit of lustfully eyeing off a woman. However, a perve is a sexual pervert.

Petrolhead
One who is obsessed by his or her car far and beyond the medallion of the Blessed Virgin and the pyjama puppy in the back seat behind the venetian blinds. One who decorates his or her car in the taste of idiocy.

Phoney

Normally used in the somewhat archaic phrase 'phoney as a two-bob watch', meaning that the person being referred to is a trickster. Always used in reference to bipeds.

Pie eater

A person of no consequence. A *dickhead*.

Pig Iron Bob

This now archaic expression refers to an obscure and more than somewhat fat leader of the Australian Federation in the 1950s and 1960s who fancied himself in double-breasted suits. His phrase-making fame came from the fact that he sold a lot of scrap iron to the Japanese empire shortly before the start of a minor matter known as World War II. The Japanese empire returned this favour in the form of shells, hence the phrase 'Pig Iron Bob'. His full name was Robert Gordon Menzies.

Pike

To pike is to opt out of something, give up easily, or leave early from an event. A 'piker' is one who might 'pike out' of a party, or back down from an arrangement.

Piss

Alcohol – much the same as *grog*. The word is also used in numerous phrases – e.g.: 'piss off' means go away, 'be/get pissed' means be/get drunk, and 'be/get pissed off' means be/get annoyed.

Piss in the same pot

The same as 'pee in the same pot' which is very nearly the same as the Americanism, 'to piss in someone's pocket'; or, to use another Americanism, in a slightly different sense, 'to have his pecker in my pocket' (Lyndon Johnson, circa 1966). In general terms to be a crawler or to suck up to someone.

Piss poor

A poor show. The horse or the *footie* team performed badly. 'Piss weak' is similar.

Piss yourself

To laugh so hard that you more or less wet your pants.

Pissed as a parrot

To be very drunk: *see* FULL AS A. 'Pissed as a newt' and '*tanked*' can also be used.

Pisspot

A drunkard.

Pitt Street Farmer

A Sydney expression which had some original sense when all the banks were in Pitt Street of that city. Means that someone is using country property losses for city advantages. The Melbourne equivalent is 'Collins Street Farmer'.

Plonk

A form of *grog;* generally cheap wine.

Pointing Percy at the porcelain

To take a leak, have a *piss*. To urinate. Similar to *draining the dragon.*

Pokies

Poker machines, known elsewhere as 'fruit machines' and 'one-armed bandits'. These coin-fed gambling monsters are extra ordinarily popular with Australian *punters,* who, it has been said, will bet on anything – even two flies crawling up a wall.

Polly/pollie

A parrot or a politician; the definitions are similar.

Pom

An English person. The origin is uncertain, with explanations ranging from POM (Prisoner of His/Her Majesty – a convict) to an abbreviation of pomegranate, rhyming slang for 'immigrant'. Well known and well-used variations include 'Pommy' or 'Pommie', 'Pommy *bastard*' and '*whingeing* Pom'.

Pommy Land

England, where all the *Poms* and 'Pommy *bastards'* come from.

Pony

A small glass that can be used for both beer and spirits.

Poofter

(derog.) A male homosexual or *shirt-lifter.*

Port

A suitcase (portmanteau) or bag. An archaic term that has died out virtually everywhere in the world except in ultra conservative Queensland.

Possum

A term of endearment, as in "You little possum, you", made particularly famous by Dame Edna Everage, a creation of the satirist and comedian Barry Humphries. Something soft and cuddly. Unfortunately Australian possums are anything but cuddly, having razor sharp claws.

Postie

A postman or postwoman.

Pot

A medium-sized beer glass, similar in capacity to a *middy*, or its contents. *See also* LADY'S WAIST.

Poultice

If one 'puts a poultice' on something one has invested a serious amount of money (usually on a horse).

Pox doctor's clerk

If one is dressed up like a pox doctor's clerk one is deemed to be overdressed, out of character, or *lairy*.

Pozzie

A spot, place or position – as in, "We're goin' to the *footie* early to get a *top* pozzie".

Prezzie

A gift or present, like you receive at *Chrissie*.

Proddy dog

(derog.) A Protestant – not a *Tyke* or a *Mick*.

Pub

A hotel – a place to drink and somewhere to stay the night.

Pull your head in

Shut up.

Punch the bundy

Literally to arrive at work on time and check in at one's appointed hour. However, in popular parlance *punching the bundy* meant that one was unwillingly doing a lot of 'hard graft' in an effort to 'make a *quid*'.

Punter

One who bets money on the horses, dogs, the *trots, pokies,* or anything else. Most Australians are punters.

Push

Recently, a literary/artistic movement, such as the 'Sydney Push' and the 'Balmain Push' of the 1960s–70s. Members of a push were once regarded as *larrikins* or 'street *stoushers*'.

Put the bite on

To ask for a loan of money.

Put the hard word on

To ask for a favour or loan, or to make (usually unwelcome) sexual advances to someone.

Put the mockers on

To wish or cause bad luck.

Q

Qantas

Everyone knows this is Australia's national airline founded in the *Outback* in the 1920s – but most people are not aware that the name is the acronym for Queensland and Northern Territory Aerial Services.

Quick snort

A hastily consumed alcoholic drink. "I've only got time for a quick snort, *mate*".

Quid

Formerly a one pound note, still occasionally heard in the phrase 'not worth a bloody quid' (worthless), or 'not the full quid' (insane).

Rabbit

Used by either males or females about another male who is held to be weak, normally in the phrase, he's a 'bit of a rabbit'. Rabbits also have the distressing tendency to 'rabbit on'; to talk about nothing at all over an interminable period of time whereupon they are told to 'stop rabbiting'. On the other hand a 'rabbitoh' (now archaic) was one who sold rabbits for a living from door to door. He was normally accompanied by a *mate* who sold clothes props which were not used to prop up clothes, but rather the line that held the said garments on washing day.

Race off

If you race someone off, you seduce them.

Rack off

Similar to *nick off,* in that it can simply mean to leave ("I'm going to rack off now"). The term can also be used as in the same way as '*piss* off' or '*bugger* off'.

Rafferty's rules

An event or contest operated with Rafferty's rules is run with no rules at all.

Rage

A sort of late-night perambulating party involving anyone from the sub-teen acne set through punks and *dole-bludging* hippies to yuppies. Normally involves grog, the acceptable social drugs of the day and a little statutory fornication. Not half as much fun as the old-fashioned *rort* or shivoo, which not only involved all of the above but serious fist fights as well.

Rapt

If one is rapt in something it is really good. Rapt can also imply that a person is infatuated with someone – e.g.: "She's totally rapt with her new boyfriend".

Rat up a rope

If one does something 'like a rat up a rope' one moves exceedingly quickly. An alternative is 'rat up a drainpipe'.

Ratbag

The *bush* version of a *dickhead*.

Rat's arse

A rat's arse is something that is worth about as much as a real rat's arse – that is, very little indeed. So using it to express an opinion enhances clarity and conciseness – as in, "I don't give a rat's arse about yer stupid *bloody* sister".

Ratshit

Something that is broken, of poor quality, or of little use can be described as being ratshit. If feeling unwell, one could also say "I'm ratshit today". 'RS' is an acceptable and commonly used abbreviation.

Rattle your dags!

An instruction to 'get moving!' *See* DAGS *for a full explanation.*

Rattler

A train. If one 'jumps the rattler' one hides in a cattle truck to avoid paying one's fare.

Raw prawn

If someone 'comes the raw prawn', one has behaved in an extremely offensive or deceiving fashion, hence, "Don't come the *bloody* raw prawn with me, *mate*".

Real dropkick

Someone who is a real *droob* or nerd (American: wimp), with the added disadvantage that he or she is probably on hard drugs.

Red Centre, The

The heart of the *Outback,* so called because of the region's predominantly reddish rocks and soil. Places such as Alice Springs, Ayers Rock (Uluru) and The Olgas (Kata Tjuta) are smack bang in the middle of The Red Centre. Similar to the *Dead Heart.*

Reds under the bed

All right-thinking middle class Australians were once terrified of finding reds (communists) either under the bed or dominating the unions and running the country. The fear actually had nothing to do with the rise of the Soviet Communist Party. Australians have constantly feared invasion by Russia since the days of the Tsar. The country's coastline is littered with useless nineteenth-century forts that were built to thwart this. This is despite the fact that the northern and frozen nation has shown no interest whatsoever in claiming Ayers Rock as its own. The now archaic phrase 'reds under the bed' was later used as a term of derision by members of the Labor Party's left wing when their political opponents *carried on like a pork chop.*

Rego
Registration, particularly the motor vehicle variety.

Rellies
One's family and relatives are commonly referred to as 'the rellies' or 'the rels'.

Ridgie didge
On the level; the *good oil*. The truth.

Righty-ho
An expression that indicates 'yes' or 'okay'. *See also* ROTARY-HOE.

Ringer
The fastest shearer in the shed. Also known as the gun or gun shearer.

Ring-in
Someone brought in as a substitute – as in, "He's just a ring-in for my usual *postie*".

Ripper
An expression of joy. If someone shouts, "You little ripper", it means that his or her horse has won the race.

Rissole
A normally circular meat or fish patty, but *see also* RSL. The word is often used as part of the friendly farewell "See you round like a rissole".

Road train
Frequently encountered in northern and *Outback* Australia, these monstrous articulated vehicles consist of a prime mover and as many as three semi-trailers.

Rocking horse shit

Something 'as rare as rocking horse shit' is extremely scarce indeed. *See also* HEN'S TEETH.

Rollie

A hand-rolled *durry*.

Roo

Abbreviation for kangaroo. 'The Roos', however, could refer to one of several *footie* teams.

Roo bar

Also known as a 'bull bar'. A piece of metal at the front of a vehicle, designed to reduce the damage caused by a collision with a kangaroo or other animal while travelling in the *bush* or *Outback*.

Room in a railway station

An unusual but not totally archaic phrase meaning that someone is down on his or her luck. The only place to sleep is in the waiting room of a railway station.

Root

As a verb, root means to have sexual intercourse, while *a* root is either one's sexual partner ("He's a great root") or the sexual act itself ("Fancy a root?"). In Australia, therefore, it is generally wiser *to barrack* rather than 'root' for your team.

Rooted

Totally exhausted *(see* ROOT *for the reason why)*, or broken, as in 'the 'fridge is rooted'.

Ropeable

Extremely angry or bad tempered.

Rort
A party with dancing and violence (and of course grog).
Also to trick or to cheat, and the act of cheating.

Rotary-hoe
A variation of *righty-ho*.

Rotten
In addition to its normal meaning of bad or offensive, rotten
implies extreme intoxication – "She got totally rotten at the
wedding reception".

Rough as guts
A bad tum, a piece of bad sportsmanship or a deliberately
nasty act, as in "Did you see what the *bastard* did? That was
as rough as guts". Also used to describe someone lacking in
social graces, a peg down the ladder from 'common'.

Rough end of the stick
Someone has had the *dirty* done on him or her and is thus
left holding the rough end of the stick.

Rouseabout

A general hand in a shearing shed.

RS

See RATSHIT.

RSL

This ex-serviceman's organisation (the Returned Services League) is best known for its clubs, complete with bars, restaurants, live entertainment and *pokies,* that are dotted all over the nation. Australians therefore often say they are off to the RSL or *rissole* for a night out.

Rubbity

An old-fashioned term, short for 'rubbity dub' – a *pub* or hotel.

Rug rat

A small and obnoxious child under two years of age. Similar to an *ankle biter.*

Rugger-bugger

A mildly offensive term for a fanatical Rugby Union supporter, used mainly by those who support the other, far more important, football codes – *Aussie Rules* and *League.*

S

Saltbush
Marginal and virtually useless sheep-grazing country invariably settled by *battlers,* such as Jolliffe's cartoon character 'Saltbush Bill'. Anyone in the *bush* who is known locally as Saltbush Bill is regarded as a failure.

Saltie
A saltwater crocodile, found in Australia's north. These specimens are big, bad and ugly. Go and meet one: you'll see *he's got a head on him like a robber's dog,* and he'll make sure you never enjoy a *dingo's breakfast* again.

Salvo
A member of the Salvation Army of either sex. A female Salvationist is sometimes called a Sally Anne.

Sandgroper
A person from Western Australia. Also a 'groper'.

Sandshoes
Canvas shoes with rubber soles, known elsewhere in the world as joggers, runners, sneakers, plimsolls, gym shoes, etc.

Sandwich short of a picnic
Used to describe someone who is a *couple of pies short of a grand final. See also* NOT THE FULL BOTTLE.

Sandy blight
An eye infection suffered by someone living in the interior of Australia. The eye disease trachoma.

Sanger

A sandwich, also known as a 'sammie' or a 'samba'.

Sarky

Bad tempered or sarcastic, as in, "Don't get sarky with me, you *bastard*".

Sav

Short for a largish dyed sausage known as a saveloy, which is a sort of inflated frankfurter or hot dog. A battered sav on a stick also known as a Dagwood dog – (for the uninitiated: a saveloy covered in a flour and water paste, impaled on a popsicle stick and then deep fried) is still an esteemed Australian fairground snack. This culinary horror is invariably dipped in tomato sauce before being thrust into the fingers of the unwary.

School

A group of people, usually men, happily settled into a session of drinking or gambling, such as *two-up*.

Schooner

A large beer glass, generally containing 425 ml. *See also* LADY'S WAIST.

Scorcher

A *bloody* hot day. A 'real scorcher' is a *bastard*.

Scratchie

A cheap lottery ticket, purchased from newsagents and scratched with a coin to discover if one has won a sum of money. This modest form of gambling is a favourite of *Aussie punters*.

Scrubber

A cow or steer that has gone wild in the scrub. Also an ugly woman, or a female with loose morals.

Scrub round it

To avoid or disregard a problem, thus, this exchange:
"Hey *mate!* the roof's about to fall in". "Don't worry *mate,*
we'll just scrub round it and *she'll be Jake* in no time at all".

Scrub up well

If one scrubs up well one is deemed by one's peers to have
managed to get dressed quite decently and look *not half bad*
after an appalling night *on the turps.* Also some women are
said by males to scrub up well, which simply means that
they have dress sense. This is merely thought and not
uttered.

Scumbag

A classic *Aussie* insult that is addressed to someone who is
despicable. The word was made particularly famous by a
1990s Labor Prime Minister, who used it regularly when
referring to certain members of the Opposition.

Scunge

Something or someone best described as unkempt or dirty.
The adjective is 'scungy', which can also imply meanness.

See yer later

A typical Australianism which does not mean that the one
who utters the phrase has any intention whatsoever of
meeting the person in question at a future date. It simply
means goodbye. Confusing to foreigners.

Selection

A land grant. Now found only in nationalistic literature and
starting with the words, "Things were *crook* on our
selection..." The worst selection in Australia was farmed by
the literary figures of Dad and Dave who were the heroic
battlers of Steele Rudd's *On Our Selection* and *On Our New
Selection.*

Servo
A service, petrol or gas station.

Shag
A verb or noun that refers to the act of sexual intercourse. Not to be confused with the 'shag' in the expression *like a shag on a rock.*

Shagged
Exhausted – from hard work or other activities *(see above).*

Shake hands with the wife's best friend
A lengthy male euphemism for the act of urination, normally prefaced by, "Hang on a minute, I'm just going to..." *See also* DRAINING THE DRAGON *and* POINTING PERCY AT THE PORCELAIN.

Sharkbait
A stupid swimmer who body surfs or swims in dangerous areas, encouraging attacks by sharks.

Sheila
A generic term for any member of the female sex. Although the word is used only by *blokes* and has become terribly clichéd, it is still heard in the *bush* and other politically incorrect circles.

She'll be Jake
An expression meaning that things are all right, which they are not. 'She's Jake' can also be used.

She'll be right
Much more commonly used nowadays than *she'll be Jake* or *she's sweet,* but also indicating that everything will turn out fine and there is absolutely no need to panic. *See also* NO WORRIES.

She's apples
Identical to *She's sweet*.

She's sweet
See SHE'LL BE RIGHT *and* NO WORRIES. 'She'll be sweet' is a variation.

Shicker
If one gets 'on the shicker' one intends to get drunk, hence shickered.

Shirt-lifter
(derog.) A male homosexual.

Shirt tearing
A form of male *pub* fighting in which no-one is intended to get hurt and no-one does. In retrospect normally spoken of with disgust. "It was just a bunch of shirt tearing".

Shirty
Someone who is being bad-tempered or irritable could be said to be shirty, which is similar to 'shitty'.

Shit-eh?
Frequently used to denote surprise or wonderment, despite the fact that it doesn't really mean anything.

Shithead
Someone who is mean and contemptible. *See also* HUNGRY BASTARD.

Shit-yeh!
A famous *Aussie* expression of enthusiastic affirmation or approval: "Did *youse* go to the *pub* last night?" "Shit-yeh! There was nothin' worth watchin' on the telly".

Shivoo
A party, similar to a *rort,* except that initially dancing takes precedence over fighting.

Shonky
Goods of poor quality or a job that has been badly done.

Shoosh
A demand for an audience to shut up, as in, "Let's have a bit of shoosh, ladies and gents".

Shoot through
To move or depart rapidly: "Look, I'm late, I'd better shoot through!' Often used when a man suddenly leaves his wife after learning of an unplanned pregnancy. *See also* SHOT THROUGH LIKE A BONDI TRAM.

Shot through like a Bondi tram
Somewhat archaic although still in use by those who remember the days of Sydney trams with affection. The Bondi tram was notoriously the most dangerous and fastest. It means therefore that the person in question has 'pissed off at the high port' or fled very quickly indeed.

Shouse
Something not very nice. Short for shithouse.

Shout
To *stand* a round in a *school* of drinkers in a *pub,* hence, "It's my shout". One whose tum it is to shout is said to *be in the chair.*

Shout for Ruth
To go for the 'big spit'. To vomit or *chunder.*

Show willing

To indicate that one is prepared to either work hard or fend for one's self as best one can. One shows willing if one is going to *crack hardy*.

Sickie

If one 'takes a sickie' one pretends one is ill while actually attending the races or going to the beach. To sadly misplace the trust and generosity of one's employer. The word has also come, however, to occasionally mean a genuine sick day.

Silvertail

A member of the upper classes or anyone who is richer than the person making the accusation. The adjective *bloody* normally precedes the use of the word.

Sin bin

A place where a sportsman is sent after being ordered off the field for appalling behaviour. *See also* BLOOD BIN.

Sit up like Jacky

To brightly and conspicuously pay attention to what one is being told. In the main, dogs and children sit up like Jacky. Adults seldom do.

Skerrick

If there is 'not a skerrick left' there is nothing. Normally spoken by people who arrive late for a beer and prawn night after everyone else has had a good time.

Skite

To boast.

Slab

A carton of beer, containing twenty-four *stubbies* or *tinnies*.

Sledge

A sporting, particularly cricketing, term. To sledge is to abuse and therefore undermine the opposition, preferably out of earshot of the umpire. The activity is known as 'sledging'.

Sleepout

A half-enclosed verandah where male guests, dogs and anyone else who *lobs* up can doss down for the night. The forerunner of the granny flat.

Smart-arse

A *wanker* who acts as if he knows far more than he actually does.

Smell of an oily rag

An expression that can be applied to a new comer to Australia if she or he works hard and does well. People who are said to be able to 'live off the smell of an oily rag' are those who sacrifice present comfort for future prosperity. An economical car 'runs on the smell of an oily rag'.

Smoko

The manual worker's morning or afternoon tea break, which is not necessarily for a smoke. Rigidly enforced by the unions, it is much frowned upon by captains of industry.

Smoodge

An attempt to ingratiate one's self. Used mainly to animals as in "Don't come smoodging round here, you'll get nothing to eat from me".

Snaffle

To pinch or thieve but in a minor and harmless fashion. One might snaffle a *sanger* from a buffet table, but one definitely steals a full bottle of Scotch.

Snag short of a barbie

Simple, or not 'all there'. *See also* BRICK SHORT OF A LOAD, COUPLE OF PIES SHORT OF A GRAND FINAL, KANGAROOS IN THE TOP PADDOCK.

Snags

Sausages, an essential ingredient at any *barbie*.

Snake's piss

Bad alcohol.

Snaky

Irritable.

Snort

A drink-see QUICK SNORT.

Sook

Someone who is timid, overly sentimental, or even a coward or wuss – such a person could be described as being 'sooky'.

Sool

To encourage one dog to attack either another dog, an animal or a person, as in, "Go on then, get into 'im, sool the *bastard*". The dog in question is encouraged to do serious injury, if not cause actual death.

Sparkie

An electrician.

Speedos

A generic term for *bathers* or a swimming *cozzie*. From the name of a famous Australian brand of swimwear.

Spew

To vomit or *chunder*. 'Spewin', however, can also indicate extreme annoyance – as in, "She was spewin' when he crashed the *ute*".

Spinner

The person tossing the coins in a game of *two-up*, an Australian gambling game once played with two copper pennies.

Spit chips

To be so annoyed that one is capable of chewing up logs of wood and 'spitting chips'.

Spit the dummy

Someone who has finally had enough and puts their foot down could be said to be spitting the dummy. One can also perform a 'dummy spit'.

Spunky

Sexy or attractive; a person with such an attribute is called a 'spunk'. The word can also mean plucky or courageous.

Squattocracy

A derisive term for the rich landowning class and the colonial landholding aristocracy.

Squiz

A quick look. An alternative to *geek* – as in "I've had a squiz at the menu but haven't decided yet".

Stand

To stand is to shout – usually a round of drinks.

Starve the lizards

An expression of amazement or incredulity. A downmarket version of the English expression 'By Jove!'

Station

In Australia a 'station' is not just a transport stop or terminus – the word often means a large farm or rural property, as in a sheep station or cattle station.

Sticks out like dog's balls
It does.

Stickybeak
An inquisitive person. One can 'have a stickybeak' or a 'sticky' at something, which generally implies being nosy or prying.

Stiff
A word that is used to indicate bad luck. *See also* YOU DON'T HAVE TO BE DEAD TO BE STIFF.

Stipe
A stipendiary steward at a horseracing meeting, who, sitting in judgment with his peers, has the ability to disqualify a jockey or warn a *punter* off the course for life.

Stir the possum
To create uproar. Normally a cute, friendly creature, a native possum sleeping in a hollow log reacts violently when poked with a stick – hence the phrase.

Stirrer
One who sets out to deliberately cause trouble and discontent. Shop floor stewards and members of the left-wing faction of the Australian Labor Party are normally branded as stirrers even if they are attempting to be quite agreeable at the time.

Stone the crows
Used in conjunction with *starve the lizards* or by itself as an expression of amazement about either good or bad events. In actuality both expressions have no meaning at all.

Stoush
A punch-up or a fight.

Strapped for cash

Short of money.

Strewth!

A short and supposedly decent form of the old English phrases, 'God's Teeth!' and 'God's Truth!' It gives the utterer the right to blaspheme without actually appearing to do so. Interchangeable with 'Jeez!'.

Strides

Trousers, as in the phrase, "Be right with you as soon as I get me strides on". *Daks* are similar.

Strike a light

An expression of little meaning usually inserted at the beginning of a sentence simply to give the speaker time to collect his thoughts as in, "Strike a light, but she's a *bloody beaut* day".

Strike me pink

The Australian version of the English, 'fancy that'. Something unusual has happened, usually pleasant.

Strine

Aussie for the Australian language.

Striya

The correct pronunciation of Australia, also known as *Down Under, Godzone, Oz* and *The Lucky Country*.

Strong

As in, "What's the strong of this?" meaning, "What in the name of hell is going on?" If used in the personal sense it is normally expressed as, "What's the strength of that *bastard?*", meaning, "What is the swine up to?"

Stroppy
Someone who is stroppy is in a bad temper.

Stubbies
A variety of men's work shorts, generally worn by labourers, construction workers and other macho types.

Stubby
A short, squat bottle of beer, containing 375 ml: larger than a *throwdown,* but much smaller than a *longneck,* and kept cool in a stubby holder. A true *Aussie bloke* always drinks directly out of the stubby, rather than from a glass. A *Darwin stubby,* however, is a much larger bottle – folks are particularly thirsty in *The Territory!*

Stunned mullet
If someone has an expression like a stunned mullet, that person is deemed to be both ugly and stupid. However, the Antipodean mullet is an excellent, if somewhat oily, eating fish.

Sunburnt Country, The
Yet another name for Australia – along with the likes of *Down Under, Godzone* and *Oz.*

Sundowner
An archaic word for the scruffier version of the normal *swaggie.* While the normal *swagman* would arrive in time to split a load of wood in order to get his *tucker* ration, the sundown er deliberately arrived at a *station* or homestead at dusk so that any thought of work was impossible.

Sunnies
Sunglasses.

Surfie
One who surfs.

Suss

To search out, thus to 'suss out'; or something suspicious or suspect – as in "That *bloke's* a bit suss".

Susso

The pre-World War II version of the dole. 'On the susso' meaning sustenance – was an expression of derision used by *silvertails,* and one of defiance by those on it. Technically, one who is receiving a government handout.

Swag

A bedroll (also known as a *Matilda*) containing one's personal possessions and carried by means of two straps – balanced on one shoulder only, with a flour sack, termed a *tucker* bag, used as a counter-balance in front. Easy to carry over long distances.

Swagman/swaggie

One who carries a *swag.* A wanderer. Not much seen walking these days as most swaggies have the brains to hitch rides on 'big rigs'.

Swan

One can either be 'on a swan or swanning around'. Swanning is loafing, although if one is swanning around one is a *swaggie.* To confuse the issue, if one *'swans* around all day' it usually means one has had an agreeable time at several different *boozers.* Swanning around at work means hiding in the *dunny.*

Swifty

To 'pull a swifty' is to perform an act of deception. Also 'swiftie'.

T

Ta
The lazy Australian way of saying 'thank you'. *See also*
THANKS.

TAB
The government-run Totalisator Agency Board, or betting
shop. There's one in every vaguely busy street and shopping
centre, and Australian *punters* throw away an inordinate
amount of money in them, betting on anything from horses
to the outcome of a *footie* match.

Tailor-made
A packet or manufactured *durry* which is purchased in its
pristine entirety, as distinct from a *rollie* which is put
together from the *makings*.

Take a powder
To *piss off*, *shoot through*, disappear in a hurry. Normally one
takes a powder when the *coppers* are after one.

Take a shine to
To take a liking to someone.

Talk under wet cement with a mouthful of marbles
Refers to a *pub* bore whom no-one can shut up.

Talk you blind
The same *pub* bore who does. An *ear basher*.

Tall poppy
Any Australian who reads more than the sporting results and knows how to use snail tongs. Someone who aspires to intellectual excellence and cannot tell the difference between one make of car and another. The species is much hated in Australia and is always being cut down to size. This last act is the main reason why the country will always suffer from intellectual cretinism.

Tank
The word used west of the Darling River in New South Wales and in the *Dead Heart,* for a dam.

Tanked
Drunk, particularly as a result of consuming too much beer.

Tassie
The island state of Tasmania, also known as *The Apple Isle.* Pronounced 'Tazzie'.

Tea
Most *Aussies* have breakfast, lunch and *tea.* Only posh people call it 'dinner'.

Technicolour yawn
To vomit. *See also* CHUNDER *and* LIQUID LAUGH.

Ten-ounce sandwich
A *liquid lunch,* which could also be described as a *Clayton's* meal.

Territory, The
The Northern Territory, featuring places such as Darwin, Alice Springs and Ayers Rock (Uluru). Home to the 'Territorians'.

Thanks

The economy of Australian English is such that *Aussies* often say 'thanks' instead of both 'please' and 'thank you'. Some examples: "Two *schooners* thanks" (when in the *pub*); "*Darlo,* thanks *mate*" (to a *cabbie*); or "I'll have fish and chips thanks" (in a restaurant). If the situation does require a 'thank you', *ta* is normally used.

That's the shot!

An expression of wholehearted approval.

The middle of the bloody day and not a bone in the truck

Nothing has been achieved despite a fair amount of striving.

Things are crook in Tallarook/Muswellbrook

Matters are not reaching any satisfactory conclusion, the times are bad and everything is *up shit creek*. Apart from that, the phrase has no meaning at all; it is just something to say during a lull in the conversation.

Thirty-seven degrees in the water bag

A hot day. One of the few successful translations from the imperial to the metric measurement of temperature, indicating that the liquid in the canvas water bag is at blood heat.

Thongs

Part of the Australian national dress, these cheap and very basic rubber sandals feature a 'thong' between the big and second toes. They are known as 'flip-flops' in the UK and 'jandals' in New Zealand.

Throwdown

A very small bottle of beer, containing a mere 250 ml. So-called because the contents can be 'thrown down' in one hearty gulp.

Tick

If one gets something on tick one is getting one's beer on the slate or on credit.

Tickets on himself

If a male has tickets on himself he is regarded as a *lairy* stuck-up *bastard*. Someone who believes himself to be smarter than he actually is.

Tickle the Peter

Someone who tickles the Peter is a minor thief. The English equivalent is a 'poor box John'.

Tiger country

Rough scrub, with strong reference to the south west of Tasmania, the last known area in Australia where the probably extinct Tasmanian tiger or thylacine was sighted.

Tight as a fish's arse

A mean *bastard* who won't lend you a *quid*.

Timid fish

Someone who does not like hard work.

Tin-arsed

Lucky, although why one who is so smiled upon by Dame Fortune should have a tin bottom is beyond understanding.

Tinned dog

A derisive expression for corned beef or mutton.

Tinny/tinnie
A can of beer containing 375 ml, the same quantity as a *stubby*. Also known as a 'tube'.

Tinny short of a six-pack
Describes someone who is simple or not quite 'all there'. *See also* NOT THE FULL BOTTLE *and* SNAG SHORT OF A BARBIE.

Tired and emotional
Blind drunk. A euphemism once much used in the press for politicians who were 'three sheets to the wind' or otherwise *pissed as parrots,* to avoid the laws of libel.

Toecutter
A standover man who literally chops people's toes off to indicate, in a jovial fashion, that they have rather stepped out of line. In the political terminology, one who is extremely ruthless.

Toey
Anxious or bad-tempered.

Togs
Clothes, particularly those worn for sporting activities or swimming – in the latter sense, interchangeable with *bathers* or *cozzie*.

Too right!
An expression that means 'certainly' and which adds emphasis to a statement – for example: "Did *youse* get a *root* last night?", "Too right I did!".

Toorak Tractor
A flash four-wheel-drive vehicle. Derived from the fashionable and expensive inner-Melbourne suburb of Toorak.

Top

Excellent, the very best – always used in conjunction with another word, such as in *Top drop* and *Top night*. Also as in, 'the party was tops'.

Top drop

A particularly good bottle of wine.

Top End

Northern Australia, particularly the northern-most regions of the Northern Territory. A resident of this indefinable region is a 'Top Ender'.

Top night

One generally has a top night in the company of friends, getting blind drunk; whereas one can get *shickered* by one's self.

Touchy as a taipan

Temperamental and unpredictable. A taipan is a particularly venomous Australian snake.

Trackie dales

The trousers, or *daks,* half of a tracksuit.

Troppo

Round the twist. Usually used of people who have gone insane – 'gone troppo' – in a tropical or sub-tropical environment.

Trots

Either diarrhoea or harness racing for horses, one of which you can't bet on at the *TAB*.

Truckle

One who drives a truck.

True blue

Genuine, the real thing; or a person who is loyal.

Tucker

Food – as in, "Your *missus* cooks *beaut bloody* tucker".

Tuckerbox

A lunch box that some damn fool of a dog sat on once near the New South Wales town of Gundagai. He was guarding this box for the return of his master. As his master was dead, the dog starved to death and the food in the box went bad. This tale of needless self-sacrifice is close to the Australian psyche, about as close as the charge of the Light Brigade is to the British. Dog, tuckerbox and Gundagai have been enshrined in a bush ballad.

Turps

If one is *'on the turps'* or 'hitting the turps', one is in the process of getting very drunk.

Two pot screamer

A cheap drunk; someone who can get as *pissed as a parrot* or as *full as a* goog on two glasses of beer.

Two-up

Once the national gambling game and played with a pair of pennies thrown into the air by a *spinner*. Now, thanks to the introduction of legalised casinos, the game is on the wane.

Tyke

(derog.) A derisory term for a Catholic; the opposite end of the religious spectrum to the *Proddy dog.* Similar to a *Mick.*

U-ey

A U-turn – see CHUCK A U-EY.

Under the weather

Crook in the guts; ill. Also a euphemism for being drunk or hung over.

Underdaks

As *daks* are trousers, it follows that these are what one wears underneath – underpants or undies.

Uni

University. "If she gets good marks, she's off to uni next year".

Unit

A flat, apartment or condominium. The full name is a 'home unit'.

Up a gumtree

On the wrong track. To follow the wrong lead and therefore finish up a gumtree.

Up shit creek

Often accompanied by '...without a paddle', this expression means that one is in deep trouble.

Up the duff

In a female sense, to be 'in the club'. Pregnant. 'Up the spout' is similar.

Up there, Cazaly

Triumphant term used by *barrackers* or supporters of the game of *Aussie Rules.* Now more or less replaced by the boring phrase, 'go for it'. The legendary footballer Roy Cazaly was particularly famous for his athletic leaps.

Up who

Short form of 'who's up who and who's paying the rent?' An expression of general bewilderment in a situation where no-one is in control and matters are entirely out of hand. 'Up yours' and 'up you for the rent' have a more abusive meaning – 'get stuffed'.

Urger

Racecourse tout or tipster. A term, generally of insult, as in, "That *bastard,* he's nothing but a *bloody* urger".

Ute

Short form of 'utility'. Before the invention of the highly expensive four-wheel-drive vehicle with computer radar, the most useful vehicle in the *bush.* By law all utes must contain at least one slavering *blue heeler.*

Valley, The
Fortitude Valley, Brisbane's Chinatown region.

Vegemite
A dark-brown yeast extract that is a popular sandwich spread. No-one from a non-British, non-Australian or non-New Zealand background would even consider eating something that smells so vile.

Vegies
Vegetables – a word Australians are too lazy to say.

Vinnies
The much-loved Australian charitable organisation – the St Vincent de Paul Society. *Aussies* often 'pop down to Vinnies' to buy or deliver second-hand clothes, household goods or furniture.

Vino
Cheap wine – plonk.

Virgin's ruin
Although held to be gin *O.S.*, in Australia, Bundaberg rum – generally known as *Bundy* – is said to do the trick.

Wag
A joker or humorous person. The verb 'to wag', however, means to be absent from something (particularly school) without permission.

Walkabout
To 'go walkabout' is to wander around on a whim. The term comes from the Aboriginal practice of nomadic wandering in the *bush* or *Outback*, but someone who has merely disappeared for a while could be said to have 'gone walkabout'.

Wallaby Track
A path to the interior of the continent taken by failures. Successful people do not walk the wallaby track, they fly over it. If someone is said to be *'on the wallaby'*, it is assumed that he is roaming the countryside looking for work.

Waltzing Matilda
Literally, to carry one's *swag* along the *wallaby track*. Also the title of a rather odd jingle that almost everyone else in the civilised world fervently believes is the Australian national anthem, rather than 'Advance Australia Fair'. Quite a number of Australians think so as well.

Wanker
The literal translation is 'mental masturbator'. Someone who is having himself on, thinks he's pretty good, and doesn't really know what he is talking about.

Water burner
A *bush* or shearer's cook.

Watering hole
One's favourite *pub*.

Weak
Short for '*piss* weak' or 'weak as cold *piss* on a plate'.
The person being referred to is a doddering idiot.

Wedding tackle
A euphemism for the male sexual organs.

Weekend warrior
(derog.) A member of the Australian Army's Reservist units.
The term is intended to be derogatory and is a variant on
'*cut lunch* commando'. Most Australian *blokes* prefer to defend
their country at weekends from the redoubts of the nearest
public bar.

Well-heeled
A 'flash *bastard*' who's got more money than sense. However,
he might be good for a 'bite' (loan).

Wellies
Wellington boots or gumboots.

Westie
(derog.) A term for someone from the western suburbs of
Sydney or Melbourne, regarded as not particularly salubrious
places to live.

Wet blanket
A killjoy.

Wet, The
The tropical rainy season in northern Australia, generally running from the months of December to April. *See also* DRY, THE.

Whack up
To share out. One 'whacks up' the proceeds that your betting syndicate has just won on the races.

Whacker
A person of no consequence; a fool.

Whacko
An expression of joy as in, "Whacko, we've just won the *slab* of beer in the *pub* raffle". Anything more whacko than whacko is 'whacko the diddle-o' or 'whacko the *chook*'.

Wharfie
Short for waterside worker. In international terms, a stevedore.

What's the damage?
"What's the cost?" or "how much do I owe?" – as in a restaurant bill, for example.

What's the strength
Roughly, what in the name of hell is happening? But it can also be a query about a person's character, as in, "What's the strength of that *bastard* over there? Is he on the level or is he just putting us on?" *See also* STRONG.

Where the crows fly backwards

'The back of beyond' or *Woop Woop*. In areas such as these the crows are forced to fly backwards to keep the dust out of their eyes.

Whinge

To whine or complain. One who whinges is called a 'whinger', a term that is often linked with *Pom. See also* GRIZZLE.

White ant

To destroy another's character by slanderous and probably truthful gossip, normally expressed thus, "I was doing all right with the *sheila* until the *bastard* white anted me".

White leghorn

(derog.) A female lawn bowler. The standard dress for a woman who is a member of a lawn bowls team is white hat, white blouse, white skirt, white stockings and white shoes. Hence she is named after the well-known *chook*.

Widgie

See BODGIE.

Who's robbing this coach?

A warning to someone to mind their own business, which comes from the rather tired *pub* joke which goes:

Ned Kelly held up the mail coach, ordered all the passengers to get down into the road and then stated, "I'm going to rob all the men and rape all the women".

One gentleman intervened and said he would be damned if the blackguard would be allowed to carry out his intentions in regard to the ladies of the company. At that point one female piped up, "Who's robbing this coach, you or Mr Kelly?'

Within cooee

Nearby, close; within calling distance (*see* COOEE). The term can also mean 'almost', as in "She was within cooee of getting that job". The opposite is: 'not within cooee'.

Wog

(*derog.*) This can be both an offensive racial description and a minor illness or disease, such as a cold – as in, "I can't come to work today, I've got the wog".

Wood duck

Technically the Australian wood duck is classified as a marred goose. Thus anyone who is called a wood duck is a goose. An idiot.

Woop Woop

Where the crows fly backwards or 'the arse end of nowhere'. Similar to the *Back o' Bourke.*

Wouldn't have a bar of it

A phrase used to describe someone's inability to tolerate an act or situation.

Wouldn't know

The start of a number of expressions, all of which mean stupidity. Thus, 'wouldn't know it from a bull's foot', 'wouldn't know if his arse was on fire', 'wouldn't know if a band were up him until he got the drum'.

Wouldn't piss on you if you were on fire

Describes someone who is extremely mean-spirited.

Wouldn't read about it

Something both unusual and unfortunate has just taken place, as in, "I thought we were *home and hosed,* but you wouldn't read about it, the boss came round the corner of the shed and caught us with the lot. Unreal, it was".

Wouldn't shout If a shark bit him

The person referred to shows a marked reluctance to *stand* his round in the public bar *school* and will seldom, if ever, *be in the chair*. A *bastard* who won't buy you a drink.

Wouldn't shout in a shark attack

Similar to *Wouldn't piss on you if you were on fire,* but also implying stupidity.

Wouldn't work in an iron lung

The person in question would indeed not. Exceedingly lazy.

Wowser

A non-drinking Christian who also attempts to get pornographic movies banned and regards the works of Shakespeare as suspect due to certain erotic passages.

Wrinklie

An old person, such as one's parents.

Wuss

A person who is timid or fearful – similar to a *sook*.

Xenophobe

A standard Anglo-Saxon *Aussie bloke,* who is also probably a *dole bludger*.

Yabber
To talk or chatter at speed; from an Aboriginal word.

Yabbie
A freshwater crayfish despised by Australians and esteemed by dirty foreigners. Also 'yabby'.

Yachtie
A keen sailor or yachtsperson.

Yacker
Work. Most work is 'hard yacker'. Also known as 'yakka'.

Yam
If one 'has a yam', one engages in conversation with another. But one can also tell or spin a yam, which means that one is a teller of tales or stories. Most yam spinners are *bloody* great liars.

Yellow Peril

An all-embracing term that once covered the hordes of Asians that were poised to storm the country and wrench it from the rightful grasp of the European Protestant invaders of the late eighteenth century. *See also* REDS UNDER THE BED.

Yobbo

Similar to a hooligan, lout or *hoon*. 'Yob' is a variation.

You beaut

See BEAUT.

You can't walk on one leg

The person who has just uttered the phrase has, after having consumed one drink, accepted the offer of a second from his kind companion. A roundabout and needlessly complicated way of saying, "Yes, *thanks*".

You don't have to be dead to be stiff

Meaning that one can have a run of bad luck under almost any circumstances and for no good reason. The word *stiff* equals bad luck. '*Stiff* cheddar, *mate*' is an Australianism for the English phrase, 'Hard cheese, old chap.' In coarser and more unfeeling circles it is sometimes translated as '*Stiff* shit, *mate*'.

You tell him, I stutter

This translates as, "I am sick and tired of attempting to explain the facts of life to this *drongo* here, so you have a go at it because I can no longer be bothered". The person who has just abandoned explaining does not stutter and has never been known to; the 'I stutter' is included simply to show total contempt.

You wouldn't be dead for quids

Something amazing and amusing (normally involving another's misfortune) has just occurred, thus making thoughts of suicide, for the time being at least, unnecessary.

You're not wrong

The Australian way of saying, 'You are right'.

You're right

The Australian version of the Americanism, 'You're welcome', which can also mean 'that's okay'. Sometimes rendered as either *She's sweet* or *No worries*. *See also* ARE YOU RIGHT?

You've got to be in it to win it

If one doesn't buy a ticket in the lottery one doesn't 'stand a show' of collecting first prize. Self-explanatory.

Your blood's worth bottling!

This might be said to someone who you admire greatly, or who has done something particularly praiseworthy.

Youse

The plural version of the singular you, as in 'see youse later', which in itself means goodbye. Youse, or 'yous', can be one person or many.

Yowie

A mythical ape-like creature, similar to a yeti, that is believed to roam the *bush* and the *Outback*.

Z

Zam-Buk
Now archaic, but formerly the name for a voluntary or paid first aid or ambulance officer of either sex present at a sporting event. From a healing cream applied to wounds.

Zonked
Dead tired. Similar to *rooted,* but generally due to hard work rather than other activities.

New Holland Publishers

Level 1, 178 Fox Valley Road, Wahroonga, NSW 2076, Australia

newhollandpublishers.com

This edition published in 2024 by New Holland Publishers

First published 1986. Reprinted 1987 (three times), 1988 (three times), 1989, 1990, 1991, 1992, 1993, 1994, 1995, 1998.

Revised edition 2000, 2010, 2012, 2013, 2014, 2016, 2018.

A record of this book is held at the National Library of Australia.

ISBN 9781760797690

Managing Director: Fiona Schultz
Designer: Andrew Davies
Production Director: Arlene Gippert
Printed in China

Keep up with New Holland Publishers:

f NewHollandPublishers

@newhollandpublishers